W9-CGY-549

"Not numbers. Not faceless individuals. Each case a person. Her dreams, his pain, her ambition, his loves, her fear, his despair. We stagger as we try to understand our nation's benefit from and yet deep fear of immigrants. This slender and uplifting volume guides us to new understandings of exactly what is at stake for our future. *A must read, as important now as ever.*"

—**MARGARET H. MARSHALL,** immigrant, and former chief justice of the Massachusetts Supreme Judicial Court

"Susan Cohen's masterful case studies of the adventures of eleven of her immigration clients are rich in detail, but the book ultimately tells a single tale, shot like an arrow: Would-be immigrants to the United States can run a gauntlet of atrocities in their countries of origin, only to encounter unreasonable obstruction later from the inaptly named 'immigration and naturalization' services of our own government.

"The stories are poignant, terrifying, and maddening, evoking pity and terror in the mode of a Greek tragedy.

"At the end of the day, however, the book is uplifting. The heartbeat of Susan Cohen's narrative is the heartbeat of the immigrants themselves, intensely grateful for the opportunity to work hard to create a secure life for themselves and their children.

"Anyone reading this book will find it a small wonder that nearly half of all 'Fortune 500' companies in the United States are led by immigrants or the children of immigrants as CEOs. By the time they raise their hand to take the oath of allegiance before a federal judge, many have passed through a crucible and have the strength and resilience of tempered steel."

—**WILLIAM WELD,** United States attorney for Massachusetts from 1981–1986, governor from 1991–1997, and a law partner of Susan Cohen.

"For renowned immigration lawyer Susan Cohen, each migrant has as a story to tell even though these stories are often tragically lost in the highly politicized immigration debate. The stories of these eleven brave people and their families are a powerful reminder that America must live up to its promise as a democratic beacon of hope for people around the world by welcoming immigrants and being a land where justice and compassion prevail."

—JOHN SANDERS, former acting commissioner,
U.S. Customs and Border Protection

"From the front lines of the fight for immigrant justice, one of the nation's leading immigration attorneys, shares the stories of courageous immigrants she helps every day. Chapter-by-chapter, story-by-story, Susan Cohen shines light on the way our antiquated and, at times, cruel immigration system treats the stranger among us."

—ALI NOORANI, executive director, National Immigration Forum

"Behind every immigrant is a human story. Susan Cohen brings these stories to life with inspiring accounts of her clients, who braved many hardships to join, and help constitute our nation of immigrants. *An essential antidote to the anti-immigrant rhetoric that too often dominates US politics.*"

—DAVID COLE, national legal director, ACLU;
author of *Enemy Aliens: Double Standards and Constitutional Freedoms in the War on Terrorism*

"Susan Cohen has written an important book full of insight, honesty and wisdom. As an experienced immigration lawyer, she speaks from the front lines. The stories she tells will move you and remind you why immigration is so vital to America's future."

—BILL BRADLEY, former United States senator

"Susan Cohen's *Journeys from There to Here* puts names and faces to the headlines we read on America's immigration and asylum problems. Too often we see only the numbers—more than 200,000 people apprehended at our southern border each month in mid-2021—but miss the actual details of who these people are, why they come, and what they contribute to America if we welcome them. Cohen introduces us to remarkable people and the hurdles they face, not just to get here but to remain in the face of open hostility from some politicians. It will make you cry and smile—but most of all it will make you proud that we are a country that offers hope and promise for so many."

—LINDA CHAVEZ, former director of public liaison in the White House under President Reagan and frequent writer on immigration issues.

"This fascinating, challenging, and stimulating book by Susan J. Cohen with Steven T. Taylor truly helps others to walk a mile in immigrants' shoes. A penetrating book with great insight and practical suggestions, *this is a must read for CEOs of corporations, religious heads, and university presidents.*"

—SUDARSHANA DEVADHAR, resident bishop, New England Conference—United Methodist Church

"In the moving and inspiring stories of these diverse immigrants—including refugees fleeing political, religious, ethnic persecution—this distinguished immigration attorney has drawn on her vast experience and wisdom to paint a haunting picture of America's dysfunctional immigration and asylum system. These stories compellingly portray the vast array of gifts and benefits that these immigrants, representative of the vast majority of immigrants to our country, have bestowed on America. And yet, the vivid depictions of their plights belie our biblical values of welcoming the stranger and show us that we must act now to improve our immigration systems and do better in opening our hearts to those seeking refuge and freedom when they come to our shores."

—RABBI DAVID SAPERSTEIN, former US ambassador-at-large for International Religious Freedom; senior advisor for policy and strategy, Union for Reform Judaism

"With remarkable clarity and unique insight, Susan Cohen's *Journeys from There to Here* offers readers an important and unusual close-up connection with eleven of her clients—their remarkable stories, extraordinary resilience, and harrowing pathways to citizenship. Emblematic of the thousands of immigrants who are essential members of our communities and our social fabric, Susan reminds that the vast majority of us are immigrants, and these immigrants' personal stories are all of ours. Having worked and lived in many of the places from which the clients featured in this book have fled, and seen first-hand the circumstances that moved them to make the painful decisions that led them to the US, I was moved by the joys and losses this book shared through intimate and informed personal narratives. Susan elegantly illustrates their remarkable resilience and integrity and their social and economic contributions to our communities and to our democratic systems and the rule of law. With her deep understanding of the intricacies of US immigration law and the dangerous politicization of their plight, she shares our outrage and most importantly leaves readers with clear actions for how each of us can engage and support immigrants' rights and those who heroically represent them at great personal sacrifice each day. *An important read for all who care about social justice and believe in our common humanity.*"

—ABBY MAXMAN, president and CEO, Oxfam America

"This magnificent book tells the lasting story of this country—the immigrant story—through a banker, scientist, philosopher, musician, social scientist, educator, and refugees from Sudan, China, and North and East Africa, and their remarkable lawyer Susan Cohen. This is a book about 'immigrants of the world' who are multicultural and grace our country with their immense talents and who chose a lawyer whose skills, dedication, and empathy transformed their lives and our citizenry."

—IRA KURZBAN, author, *Kurzban's Immigration Law Sourcebook*; former president, American Immigration Lawyers Association

"Susan Cohen's narratives, from the first to the last, no doubt will inspire lawyers to step up and take on immigration cases pro bono. But the true resonance of her words is found in how she opens minds and hearts to the myriad ways in which immigrants strengthen our country. *Journeys from There to Here* reminds us that while our country may provide immigrants with opportunity, it is the immigrants themselves who give our country the opportunity to be a nation of promise, hope, and limitless potential."

—JUDY PERRY MARTINEZ, past president,
American Bar Association, 2019–2020

"The captivating portraits in *Journeys from There to Here* serve as a powerful reminder that immigrants from all faith backgrounds and all walks of life strengthen America with their talents, their diversity, and their love for this country. This is a *must-read* book for anyone who wants to truly understand the American immigrant experience from start to finish in all its richness and complexity. America's greatness is found in peace, justice, unity, and coexistence for all."

—IMAM SHEIKH SA'AD MUSSE ROBLE,
founder and president, World Peace Organization

"Recounting the formidable journeys of several of her immigrant clients, distinguished Boston attorney, Susan Cohen, brings to light the pitfalls of our archaic, haphazard, and often painfully sluggish immigration system. At times both heartbreaking and joyous, Cohen beautifully recounts the implicit exceptionalism, strength, resilience, and determination of those who seek a safer and more prosperous life in America, while allowing readers a glimpse into a uniquely exhausting, life-altering legal process. Demonstrating impressive expertise and remarkable compassion, Cohen weaves striking immigrant stories with a timely reminder about what it means to be a welcoming America."

—KRISTIE DE PEÑA, vice president of policy and
director of immigration, Niskanen Center

"These stories are a 360-degree telling of the immigration journey, enriched throughout by the clear-headedness and extraordinary sympathy of the author. The 'human face of immigration' shines through on every page."

—R.H. REESE, co-founder, City of Asylum, Pittsburgh

JOURNEYS

FROM

THERE

TO HERE

STORIES *of* IMMIGRANT TRIALS, TRIUMPHS, *and* CONTRIBUTIONS

SUSAN J. COHEN

with STEVEN T. TAYLOR

RIVER GROVE
BOOKS

This publication is designed to provide accurate and authoritative information in regard to the subject matter covered. It is sold with the understanding that the publisher and author are not engaged in rendering legal, accounting, or other professional services. Nothing herein shall create an attorney-client relationship, and nothing herein shall constitute legal advice or a solicitation to offer legal advice. If legal advice or other expert assistance is required, the services of a competent professional should be sought.

Published by River Grove Books
Austin, TX
www.rivergrovebooks.com

Copyright © 2021 Susan J. Cohen

All rights reserved.

Thank you for purchasing an authorized edition of this book and for complying with copyright law. No part of this book may be reproduced, stored in a retrieval system, or transmitted by any means, electronic, mechanical, photocopying, recording, or otherwise, without written permission from the copyright holder.

Distributed by River Grove Books

Design and composition by Greenleaf Book Group
Cover design by Greenleaf Book Group
Author photo copyright by © 2021 Linda Haas Photography
Interior Image: Torch icon made by Freepik from Flaticon.com
Cover Image by Brandon Mowinkel on Unsplash.com

Publisher's Cataloging-in-Publication data is available.

Print ISBN: 978-1-63299-487-5

eBook ISBN: 978-1-63299-488-2

First Edition

For MWK

CONTENTS

ACKNOWLEDGMENTS

Writing this book has been a labor of love, a poignant walk down the memory lane of my career, and an opportunity to reflect on the contributions and support of everyone who helped me bring the book to fruition.

This book would not have come to fruition without the collaboration of my cowriter, Steve Taylor. Conceiving of and writing it together has been gratifying and meaningful. I greatly value Steve's insights, his writing prowess, and his enthusiasm for this project. Most importantly, Steve's passion and commitment to revealing and showcasing the formidable legal hurdles and the invaluable contributions of immigrants to the United States have shone throughout our work together.

My husband, Michael, and my sons, Gabe and Noah, have always been enthusiastic supporters of my immigration law career. They've been there for me, buoying me through the low points in my cases and cheering for me through the high points, graciously welcoming the clients I brought home and patiently listening to my war stories, even though, most of the time, I could not reveal who my clients were, to protect their confidentiality. Michael is my better half, my best friend, and a talented editor to boot. My love and gratitude for my family know no bounds.

This book is about my clients and my law career, and I could not have accomplished any of the work described in the book without the immense contributions of my work family. I owe so much of my success to my work better half, Ellen Wilkins, my stalwart assistant for the last twenty years. Ellen is indefatigable and a powerhouse of determination and efficiency. She has a heart of gold and is a fierce champion and supporter of all of our clients. I can think of no one better than Ellen to attend to the front lines and the phone lines for our clients. I simply could not succeed without Ellen, and all of my legal victories are Ellen's victories as well.

Some of the cases described in this book go back over thirty years. Over the decades, a small army of Mintz lawyers, legal assistants, project analysts, interns, librarians, office services staff, finance staff, marketing and public relations staff, and others have contributed in outsize ways to the successes of these cases. Specifically, I would like to extend my sincere gratitude to the following Mintz employees (past and present) who worked at one point or another on the cases of the clients we have profiled: Bill Coffman, Angel Feng, Grant Sovern, Tulio Capasso, Marisa Howe, Jeannie Smoot, Yana Dobkin Guss, Laurie Hauber, Adrienne Walker, Jeff Goldman, Danielle Lifrieri, Adrienne Darrow, Matt Hurley, Ella Shenhav, John Nucci, Emma Follansbee, Ana Lopez, Juan Steevens, Cassie Ramos, Michelle Frangella, Lorne Feinberg, Christine Bazzinotti, Eduardo Gonzalez, Gabe Santos, James Mealey, Lucy Walsh, Jenn Irving, Hilary McGregor, Venita Kaushik, Marilyn Kamuru, Molly O'Shea, and Lauren Watford. If I have inadvertently omitted any other contributors, please know I sincerely thank everyone who worked behind the scenes on these cases. They all contributed enormously to the successes of the cases described in this book. In addition, I would like to thank everyone who has worked in our Immigration Section for their earnest support, enthusiasm, and assistance with brainstorming and legal reality checks.

Many of the clients featured in this book have been pro bono clients. I can't say enough about the values that my law firm *lives* every day, including its commitment to giving back to the communities in which we operate, and its unflagging support and significant financial commitment to our pro bono program. I owe a huge debt of gratitude to our chair, Bob Popeo, and our managing partner, Bob Bodian, for their commitment to our robust pro bono program; to Sue Finegan, who tirelessly and brilliantly chairs our Pro Bono Committee; and to the past chairs of that committee, John Regier and John Markey. I would also like to thank everyone at Mintz, past and present, who has served on our Pro Bono Committee; it has been an honor to serve with them and to witness their compassion and commitment to helping those in need. I will always have a special place in my heart for Richard Mintz, of blessed memory, who embodied the firm's commitment to pro bono work and after whom our annual pro bono award is named.

I would be remiss if I did not express my deep appreciation to Mintz former managing partners Fran Meaney, Irwin Heller, and Ken Novack for believing in my wild idea of founding and growing an immigration practice at our law firm—something practically unheard of in the 1980s. I still marvel that my law firm's management gave a very junior associate the chance to turn this dream into a reality. I also owe a huge debt to my former partner Stan Twarog, who took me under his wing when I first decided to specialize in immigration law; his enthusiastic support and mentorship meant so much to me.

I also wish to thank my partners Tony Mulrain, Michael Gardener, and Pat Sharkey for their valuable advice and guidance regarding the legalities of writing a book about our clients.

All of my pro bono asylum cases have been referred by the Political Asylum/Immigration Representation Project (www.pairproject.org), known as PAIR, an absolutely extraordinary nonprofit organization that serves thousands of asylum-seekers in Massachusetts, vetting their cases to make sure they are bona fide, matching them up with lawyers who can take the cases on pro bono, and handling the cases they cannot place in house. PAIR Executive Director Anita Sharma and her predecessors, Sarah Ignatius and founding Executive Director Susan Akram, have been, and continue to be, steadfast champions for PAIR's clients, enthusiastic ambassadors for PAIR's work, and fierce champions of the legal rights of immigrants. Working with PAIR's incredible staff and clients has been the most significant and meaningful work of my legal career.

Others I wish to thank and applaud are all the caring immigration lawyers who work tirelessly every day to fight for and defend immigrants and the bar associations and nonprofit organizations that support immigration lawyers and champion immigrants' rights. Immigration law is tremendously complex, and, with few exceptions, the immigration bar, especially the members of the American Immigration Lawyers Association and the American Bar Association, is a collegial, collaborative, and closely connected group of lawyers. I would never have been able to succeed as an immigration lawyer without the mentorship and support of the immigration lawyers across the U.S. and abroad who came before me and who have offered up their time, their wisdom, and their insights to help me better serve my clients.

I also thank my friends and fellow champions for immigrants at the ACLU, both in Massachusetts and throughout the United States. And to all the other lawyers and staff across the country in civil and human rights organizations and in private practice who stand up for immigrants and fight for them, I salute you and thank you for your work.

Another unsung but very important group includes the U.S. senators, members of Congress, and their tireless immigration staffers throughout the country who devote themselves to helping their constituents overcome the formidable immigration obstacles they face in seeking to reunite with their family members, secure desperately needed American medical assistance, and solve countless other immigration roadblocks. I have so much admiration for these hardworking, compassionate patriots, and none more than Emily Winterson, now retired, whose praises I sing in this book.

While some of the clients profiled in this book suffered mistreatment by our government, I wish to emphasize that many fine and honorable public servants work in our immigration agencies. Of all the government officers and employees I have interacted with over my lengthy immigration career, Ellen Gallagher stands out for her empathy, compassion, and determination to right government wrongs when they are called to her attention. She has worked as an attorney within USCIS for decades. She has always seen each immigrant not as a faceless case number but as a human being with a beating heart, deserving of the same fair treatment and respect the rest of us desire. I salute Ellen for her tireless work to bring justice and due process to our immigration programs and systems and for understanding the precariousness of the immigrant experience.

Finally, I wish to thank all of my clients for the honor of serving and representing them. Time and time again, I am struck by the fortitude and resilience these clients have shown in the face of seemingly insurmountable odds; by their capacity for and willingness to work hard and contribute in every way they can to our country and their local communities; by their love of learning and the value they place on education; by their grace, humor, patriotism, and passion for the United States. Our country and our culture are enriched and better off because they are here. It has been the honor of my life to fight for them and their American dreams.

THE HUMAN FACE OF IMMIGRATION:

IMMIGRANTS STRENGTHEN THE SOUL OF OUR NATION

On a cold New England Saturday night in late January 2017, the day after then-President Donald Trump issued an executive order banning immigration from seven Muslim-majority nations, I wanted nothing more than a short reprieve from my hectic immigration law practice. I had looked forward all week long to attending my close friend's sixtieth birthday party and seeing her have fun. I also wanted to let loose on the dance floor.

But at the party, I was distracted and couldn't fully enjoy celebrating with my friends and my husband. I had to keep checking my phone for any urgent incoming news.

I'd previously warned the host that I might have to leave early and abruptly, but when the DJ played the first song, I was able to unwind, kick off my shoes, and move to the music. By the time the second song started, partygoers had flooded the dance floor, and you could feel the electricity of celebration. Like everyone else, it seemed, I lost myself in revelry, happy for my friend's joyous occasion with all of her close friends gathered together for her milestone birthday.

When that song ended, I realized I'd better check my phone and, sure enough, I had a message: "Come immediately to the airport." Without a moment's hesitation, I said hasty goodbyes and dashed out of there, knowing that good people were being detained at Boston's Logan International Airport and in desperate need of legal representation to fight for their rights.

My partner Sue Finegan and I, along with several other colleagues at the Boston-based law firm Mintz Levin, knew that people from some of those seven nations had boarded flights to Boston; several of them were lawful permanent residents, including professors at the University of Massachusetts. They were unaware of the executive order signed late the night before and were at-risk travelers who might be turned away because of that unjustified, xenophobic directive from the White House. They needed our protection.

Our team, along with our tightly organized small band of Boston immigration and civil rights lawyers, received word that a request for an emergency judge had been honored and the judge would preside over the matter at a federal court. So I scrambled to put on my shoes and rushed out, headed for Logan Airport. But first, I made a quick stop at my house on the way to the airport. I zipped into my driveway, left the car running with the door open, ran into my house, changed out of my high heels and into a pair of sensible shoes, and grabbed a blazer to cover up the sexy, low-cut party dress I was wearing. I didn't want to go into court and stand before the judge wearing an inappropriate outfit. I threw the jacket over my dress, sprinted back out to the car, and raced to Logan.

En route, I received a call from my colleague Sue, who was leaving the airport and said that everyone was meeting at the courthouse. I changed course, drove to the courthouse, parked illegally, and ran inside. I was sure my car would get towed away during that long night—but it wasn't. I spotted it, right where I parked it, as I walked out of the courthouse at two o'clock in the morning in exhilaration because we'd secured a temporary restraining order (TRO) enjoining the enforcement of Trump's executive order.

While I have more than three decades of immigration law practice under my belt—I created and oversee Mintz Levin's immigration group—that rush to the courthouse was just the official beginning of my advocacy to protect people from the Muslim Ban, as it came to be called. For the next several months, I worked hard, as did other passionate lawyers at Mintz and in the Boston legal community, including, importantly, at the Massachusetts office of the ACLU, to help those it affected as the situation took many twists and turns, with various courts ruling on the legitimacy of that executive order. Although our TRO was short-lived, ultimately, through vigorous and persistent advocacy, we were able to successfully defend and secure the rights of many of those immigrants.

Unfortunately, many others were subjected to the travel ban because, ultimately, the Trump administration was able to sustain the ban throughout his presidency, despite scores of legal scholars maintaining that it was unlawful and unconstitutional. As one of his first executive acts on his first day in office, January 21, 2021, President Joe Biden overturned the ban.

Fueling Anti-Immigrant Fever, Shredding the Fabric of the Nation

That executive order was, of course, the first in a string of anti-immigrant executive orders and policy changes by the Trump administration, several of which were notoriously cruel, heartless, and, many of us believe, inhumane and downright un-American. The administration detained refugees from Latin America at our southern border—in cages—and separated families. Trump and his team engaged in an all-out assault against immigrants they suspected might not be in the country legally, rounding up and detaining in prison as many people as they could find, even if they were married to U.S. citizens and had U.S. citizen children, and even if their only violation was overstaying a visa or driving with an expired registration.

Trump called for the end of chain migration (the process of an immigrant or U.S. citizen sponsoring a close relative for a green card) as if it's a bad thing, despite family reunification's long status as a cornerstone of our immigration policy (and even though the parents of the former president's wife Melania were benefactors of chain migration); tried to bar immigrants too poor to afford health insurance; forced quotas on immigration judges and eliminated their ability to exercise discretion to decide cases—for the first time in history; reduced the U.S. acceptance of refugees to a bare trickle—the lowest level since the enactment of our Refugee Law in 1980; effectively gutted our refugee program, leaving thousands of already approved refugee families to languish overseas in refugee camps; changed the mission statement of the USCIS so that visa applicants would no longer be referred to as *customers* or *stakeholders* in their immigration process—but rather, simply as *aliens*, a legal term that's used like a weapon to dehumanize immigrants. And the list goes on and on.

In all, the Trump administration carried out (or tried to carry out) more than four hundred drastic and draconian policy and regulatory changes to squeeze immigrants out of the United States and to make every type of immigration process as painful as possible.

The ex-president's policy changes and vitriolic rhetoric fueled the growing anti-immigrant movement that, in essence, encouraged violence against those who have come here from other countries. Additionally, despite Trump's election defeat, sadly, too many people, both inside and outside of government, continue to hold hateful beliefs and spew abhorrent words, which lay the foundation for harmful, often deadly, attacks on immigrants.

Immigration law in the United States is considered the most complex area in which to practice, along with tax law. On the legal front, the immigration system historically has proved to be a difficult-to-navigate labyrinth of complexities. This is true even for lawyers like me who have extensive experience with the operations of all the immigration agencies within the Department of Homeland Security, including Immigration and Customs Enforcement (ICE), Customs and Border Protection, and U.S. Citizenship and Immigration Services (USCIS). Even those of us who spend our daily lives examining the immigration statutory and regulatory framework at macro and micro levels, at times, still find our immigration laws painfully complex. Just imagine how much more over-whelming it is for immigration candidates. The requirements are fraught with administrative hoops to jump through. A lot of hoops. One little misstep, and immigration applicants could become deportable when they would otherwise have been eligible to stay. A wide range of little things can go wrong with their cases. People can easily make a mistake them-selves or rely on someone who willfully or ignorantly commits an error.

While the multistep process to enter, work, and live in the United States was arduous before one-term President Trump's tenure, it became much more difficult after he assumed office, with door after door slammed shut. The administration systematically ripped apart immi-gration protections, almost on a daily basis. Fewer and fewer people qualified for the immigration statuses and benefits to which they should be entitled—and it's not easy to reverse all of these and many other drastic changes made by the Trump White House, despite the change in administration. The reduction in immigration unravels the very fab-ric of the nation—a nation that's stronger when immigrants are able to contribute and weaker when they're unnecessarily locked out. At a policy level, it's very important to understand that individual actions by government agencies at the behest of a particular administration can kneecap immigration and reduce diversity across the country from coast to coast and border to border.

Embracing Inclusivity through Cross-Cultural Exposure

At a human interest and cultural level, it's also very important to get to know immigrants and their stories. Often, when we meet or even learn about people unlike ourselves, we unveil another side of our own humanity. It can be enlightening. A friend of mine told me a story from his childhood that he thinks truly helped shape his worldview, which he says is an experience he recalls vividly because of its cultural and philosophical import:

"When I attended elementary school in rural Illinois, a new boy of Greek heritage moved to town and entered my third-grade class. Tony Diakos (not his real last name) spoke English but not fluently, and his parents spoke very little English at all. Tall with olive skin, full dark eyes, and as sweet a kid as you'll ever meet, Tony wanted to fit in and make friends. But most of my classmates—who had lived sheltered lives and had never met a Greek person—rejected him. Worse, they bullied Tony every day at recess.

"While I saw that he was different, I was nice to Tony, partially because my parents taught each of their children to bring kids into our circle—especially those who needed friendship.

"Tony asked me to come see him perform at a graduation of sorts from a program at a Greek community center in a larger city near Chicago. I guess his parents conveyed, in halting English, to my mom and dad the details about this event and how much it would mean to Tony if I attended. I was the only kid he invited because I was his 'only friend,' they said. I had no idea he considered me his friend. And honestly, I didn't really want a friendship with him.

"The ceremony took place on a Saturday when I wanted to play baseball with my friends or go to the movies or do anything but go to the Greek center for some stupid foreign thing. My parents, however, insisted the three of us go there to support Tony and his family.

"When we arrived at the colorfully decorated venue, it seemed to radiate a sense of joy, warmth, and celebration. Here, I learned how different and delicious Greek food is as I discovered the wonders of spanakopita, hummus, tzatziki, and sweet, flaky baklava! A band played music like none I'd ever heard before, and then Tony and several other kids, all brightly costumed, performed a beautifully choreographed dance. And that's when he first spotted me. His face lit up, and I'm sure mine did too. I saw Tony not as a bullied kid with a funny accent but, rather, in his element, as an amazing and athletic dancer.

"I got a little smarter that day. My eyes opened wide, and I like to think my heart did too. Thanks, Mom and Dad. And thanks, Tony."

A Book of Success Stories

My friend continues to embrace cultural differences, and he largely attributes that to the seminal experience with foreign-born Tony and his friends and family at that vivacious, life-affirming ceremony.

I've long believed in the power of introducing someone to a person from a different country and culture to change perceptions. He or she is meeting a human being and not a stereotype, and that makes all the difference. I've held these thoughts for many years, but since the Trump presidency—with its hateful words and deeds—my feelings have grown even stronger about this. Many people spew hateful lies and unsubstantiated generalizations about immigrants, like for example that they're takers and not givers. Yet many of those same people have never met an immigrant, or else they have and they didn't realize it, or they avoid immigrants and won't engage them in conversation. Consequently, they never get to know them.

This book serves as my attempt, in a small way through storytelling, to create human connections between the reader and some of the immigrants and their families who I've been fortunate to have represented. I also hope it helps people recognize how important immigration is to our nation. While I have limited myself to sharing the stories of eleven of my clients, the immigrants featured in this book, while of course unique and remarkable, are representative of countless other clients of mine and of so many millions of immigrants to our nation in their integrity, patriotism, love of education, economic contributions, commitment to their local communities, and to our democratic system of government.

In the chapters that follow, I convey the narratives of these eleven clients. They're so much more than clients to me, because I can't help but connect with them and often remain friends with many of them long after my work on their behalf is over. I also include a brief analysis of the legal impediments my clients and I encountered and the strategies we used to navigate past the obstacles so they could stay in the United States.

In essence, this is a book of stories: the story of a seven-year-old Asian girl who was a violin virtuoso when she and her family first came here and who ultimately went on to become a world-renowned musician; the story of a Harvard-trained Honduran educator who's one of the United States' most gifted innovators in multicultural education; the story of a newly minted PhD political economist who sought asylum after fleeing his native nation in Asia to escape threats against his life by antigovernment fundamentalists because he established schools and stood up for the rights of girls and women in his home country; an Oxford- and MIT-trained Egyptian computer scientist who has revolutionized digital technology so that it can recognize human emotion; and other people who are brilliant and talented high-level professionals.

This book also features people who work in more everyday jobs, including one who bravely serves on the health-care front lines—including, of course, during the COVID-19 pandemic—those who simply wanted a better life away from the plight, poverty, and danger of their home countries. They work hard, live happy lives with their families, and contribute to the economy, culture, and well-being of communities across the United States. Some of the people showcased in these pages asked to protect their identity, for different reasons, including ongoing threats to their lives or those of their families. To honor their requests, I have used pseudonyms for their names and, at times, obscured their countries of origin.

My friend tells his story about Tony and how it influenced his worldview. I grew up listening to stories my parents told around the dinner table, which shaped my thinking as well—and probably also influenced my choice of career and my approach to serving clients. They talked about how we were one of the first Jewish families to move to our white suburban town in New Jersey. When my mother and father first drove around town looking for houses with the real estate agent, they asked him if there were many Jewish families in the town. Not knowing my parents were Jewish and interpreting their question differently than how they intended it, he said, "Oh no, you don't have to worry about that."

My parents also talked about waking up one morning to find a burning cross in our backyard, as well as other experiences that cast them as outsiders.

My family was always politically conscious and active. I grew up studying the Civil Rights Movement and was much appalled by everything I knew and had learned about the oppression of minorities in this country and also in other countries. Because of this and other experiences, I developed a strong sense of right and wrong and the importance of justice. Pursuing justice in the world and working to repair the world are also cornerstones of my faith background. With this upbringing, I became motivated at an early age to work hard to right wrongs, and I take as many steps as I can to correct injustices. This developmental background has informed my character and career and motivates me to do everything I can to help my clients.

An Injustice: Deporting a Beloved Teacher

While my team and I have achieved many victories on behalf of our clients, sometimes matters are out of our control, and despite doing everything we can, we can't help them enter or stay in the United States. Those experiences rip my heart open.

Consider the headline-making case of my client Obain Attouoman, a math and special education teacher. In the 1990s, Obain fled his native Ivory Coast after the insurgent political party issued serious threats to him because of his activism in a teachers' union. He came to the United States on an exchange visa and sought political asylum, fearing that his life would be in jeopardy if he returned to Africa.

For years, Obain taught in a private high school in Boston, where his students, fellow teachers, and administrators loved him and praised his teaching abilities. One day in 2005, while he was driving, the police pulled him over, ran a check, and learned that he had an outstanding warrant because he had accidentally missed a court date years previously. He had no idea that there was this blemish on his record. The police arrested him and threw him in jail until he could be deported. That's when leaders in the school approached me to see if I could help him. Of course, I said I'd do what I could.

My team and I explored all of the options, laid out a legal strategy, encouraged protests on his behalf, and alerted the press to bring attention to his case. We worked with the mayor of Boston at the time, Thomas Menino, and other public servants to see what they could do on our behalf. Senators Ted Kennedy and John Kerry introduced a private immigration bill to grant Obain permanent residency—but it required congressional approval, and Congress never voted on the bill. Still, we were able to get him released from jail and back into the classroom where he belonged. I continued to represent him, and he dutifully reported to the local immigration office every six months. We knew, however, we faced the high likelihood that, one day, his number would be up, so to speak, and trouble would surface.

Sure enough, one day in 2008, during one of his routine check-ins, immigration officials took Obain into custody. Despite the valiant efforts by me, my team, and others both in the courtroom and in the court of public opinion—we got a lot of press coverage, including on national television and in front-page articles in *The Boston Globe,* among other newspapers—we lost the battle. Obain was put on a plane in May 2008 and sent back to the Ivory Coast. The community was devastated, and so was I. I felt very sad for him and all of his students who thought the world of him and, of course, I also felt disappointment in the system and in myself.

All in, All the Time

Like many immigrants, Obain was law-abiding, smart, industrious, involved in his community, and grateful to live and work in this country. In my experience, immigrants are among the hardest-working people I've ever met, some holding multiple jobs, and so many instill in their children a strong work ethic, love and respect for education, and high ethical values.

Because of these attributes and the many ways in which they enrich our nation, I'm so proud to be an immigration lawyer. Of course, it's not an easy job, and I hold myself to the highest of standards. I feel very responsible for everyone who turns to me for help, and I tend to internalize a lot of anxiety, because I'm so worried on each client's behalf.

It's a huge relief both for the clients and for me when I break down the calculus of their problem, craft and implement the winning strategy, and fix their situation, which only brings us closer together emotionally. Many times, a client will say to me, "I'm so scared. Are they going to take me away?" And, invariably, I respond, "I'm going to do everything in my power so that won't happen." I take on these huge burdens for people and work hard for them because winning their cases and helping them hold on to their American dream is what keeps me going every day. It may come as a surprise to learn that thousands of caring immigration lawyers across our great country shoulder enormous emotional and mental burdens precisely because the stakes in immigration law are so incredibly high. It's not only the clients who are stricken by anxiety about their cases.

In the ensuing chapters, I tell my clients' remarkable stories and describe the many contributions they make to their communities, which I believe helps demonstrate just how important immigrants are to this country. I also offer a glimpse into some of the strategies I used on my clients' behalf. Many of the immigration cases are quite complex, but when we prevail, which we've done often, our victory celebrations are always so joyous.

SLOVAKIA

SWITZ.

AUSTRIA

HUNGARY

SLOVENIA

CROATIA

BOSNIA &
HERZEGOVINA

SERBIA

MONTENEGRO

NORTH MACEDONIA

ITALY

GREECE

ALBANIA

CHAPTER 1

EMBODIMENT OF IMMIGRANT PSYCHE:

FAMOUS WRITER FORCED OUT OF ALBANIA
AND GREECE CONTRIBUTES TO U.S.

Gazmend Kapplani stood defiantly with a dozen others at the border between their Albanian homeland and Greece, staring down four armed guards with guns drawn and aimed at them. For five long minutes on that cool evening in 1991, the two sides faced off in dead silence—that is, except for the loud panting of a fierce, highly trained German shepherd, held back by one of the border guards.

As agents of a brutal totalitarian regime in this European nation, the border officer in command and his three sharp-shooting soldiers routinely shot and killed anyone trying to cross into Greece—unless they had the regime's permission, which very few did. Any attempt to escape was considered high treason against the homeland, and the regime demanded all its border guards to obey these shoot-to-kill orders—or face a similar fate themselves.

Considered an enemy of the regime for leading antigovernment rallies in his hometown of Lushnje, twenty-four-year-old Gazi (as he's known to his friends) had been forced into hiding a few weeks earlier after learning that the state's secret police were committed to arresting, torturing, and possibly killing him. On this day, he had already taken an hours-long ride over horribly bumpy roads, hidden in the back of a truck as his friends smuggled him to the periphery of the border zone just a short distance from the checkpoint. He and his allies had gotten out of the truck in a small town and were about to embark the rest of the way on foot to attempt to cross the border into Greece. Rumors had been circulating that, like in other communist countries after the fall of the Berlin Wall, the government was crumbling, and the guards might not be there, or if they were, they might let them pass.

"When my friends had decided to smuggle me out of the country, they'd heard that the border guards don't shoot at you anymore," Gazi recalls. "The regime was collapsing, and now the normally sealed-tight borders were closed and opened often. The border guards were receiving contradictory orders. Some people in the regime told the guards, 'Don't shoot the people if they want to cross the border.' Others told them, 'Shoot the people.' They were confused and didn't know what to do. They were also afraid that if they shot people when the regime was falling apart, they might be held accountable and prosecuted."

As Gazi and his friends walked down a narrow street that led to the border checkpoint, they came upon several others who also intended to flee the country, which surprised Gazi. "We thought we'd be alone in trying to cross the border," he says, adding that his small group asked the others if the border was open and if they knew if these guards were directed to shoot anyone attempting escape.

"They said, 'If they dare to shoot us, let them shoot us,'" Gazi recalls. "Like us, they were all unarmed. That was the moment that I realized the regime was just about over. People had no fear of the border guards anymore. These people were like me: Crossing the border was the ultimate symbol of being free."

Gazi says most people in his home country had never even seen the border crossing or the barren zones around it. The regime stripped a few kilometers of the land in front of the borders of any vegetation, in many cases denuding long narrow stretches of forest. This offered guards open views of any potential escapees so they could easily aim their rifles, open fire, and drop their targets. They scorched the earth so badly that, after thirty years, the natural landscape still hasn't recovered in these zones. "All of the communist regimes had a strange obsession with borders," Gazi says. "My country was the most obsessive of all and was reduced to a totally isolated small country with the tightest of borders."

The government also took other measures to limit any successful crossings and essentially funneled vehicle and foot traffic into the checkpoints. "We were told that the scorched zones and fields around the checkpoints had landmines planted beneath their surfaces," Gazi says.

As Gazi and the others approached the border crossing, the officer yelled at them: "Where are you going?"

"We said, without offering a reason, 'We want to cross the border,'" Gazi recalls, adding that the officer asked if they had permission.

"We said, 'No, we don't need any permission. This is our border. We're humans. Humans cross borders.'"

The officer responded forcefully, "According to the rules of our state, we shoot people if you try to cross the border without permission. I order you to go back."

And that's when everyone went silent. Gazi wondered if the guards would indeed open fire if he and his companions tried to cross. "I was in the front of the line and could see the other side of the border," he says, "and, at that moment, I had a heroic thought enter my mind. *I'll be a hero. They'll say that I was killed when I was trying to cross the border.* But then fear washed over me. If the officer had given an order to the soldiers to fire, they would have killed us. But he didn't know what to do."

Looking directly at the officer, Gazi could see both anger and confusion in his eyes. His face looked pale. He seemed deep in thought. But after those five quiet, tense minutes, with the German shepherd ready to pounce, he ordered the soldiers to put down their guns and said to the small crowd, "Okay, you can cross the border. You can go."

Hearing that, they sprinted toward the barbed wire fence that separated the two countries, still fearful for their lives. "I was afraid they might kill us by shooting us in the back," Gazi says, noting that the group navigated the barbed wire and crossed a stream with waist-high, frigid water. "I remember the cold water and then I found myself on a hill with all of us laughing and shouting, 'Wow, we crossed the border! We crossed the border! We did it!' It was a moment that defined my life. When I crossed the border, I had this feeling of deliverance and freedom and living as a normal human being."

Gazi pauses after relaying those frightening but also euphoric memories, shakes his head, and, demonstrating his dry wit, adds, "Often, I wished I lived a more boring life."

He stayed in Greece for nearly a quarter-century, building a large following as a journalist, a writer, and an influential voice for immigrants around the world. But then dangerous circumstances forced his departure.

An Influential Voice and "Human Bookstore"

Gazi grew up in a small town in the middle of a plain in his mountainous native nation and in a family that had been harshly persecuted by the totalitarian government. Members of his father's side were part of the nation's old aristocracy, had gained a fair amount of wealth, and owned quite a bit of land. But the regime drove them out of their homes and confiscated their wealth and many of their possessions, even their family photos. "So, in essence, their visual memory had been erased," Gazi says. "I was born with my back against the wall because I was born in a shack, living in two small rooms with my parents, grandparents, aunts and uncles and cousins, eleven family members in all. And I grew up with a sense that I belonged to a family that was an enemy of the regime."

Sadly, Gazi's grandfather and another older family member died in that shack and were never able to experience freedom again.

When he was five years old, his parents managed to put together enough financing to be able to move into a one-story brick house in a diverse, low-income neighborhood, where Gazi heard for the first time languages different from his native tongue. He was fascinated hearing other kids speak "foreign words." That fascination piqued his curiosity and laid the motivational foundation that helped him learn the five languages he speaks today: English, French, Greek, Italian, and, of course, the language of his homeland. Looking back all these years later, he's impressed that the small community not only tolerated the language and cultural differences but embraced them—despite the militant nationalism and propaganda the nation's communist government espoused.

Around the perimeter of the plain on which Gazi's hometown sat were labor camps where the regime sent its enemies, most of whom were intellectuals. The town was affected "in a very mysterious way" by their presence, and it attracted writers, artists, philosophers, and other smart, creative people, Gazi says. "It had a very thriving cultural underground."

In his high school years, Gazi saw a solitary figure walking alone on the main avenue of town, dressed in black clothes and usually carrying a red rose—an unusual sight that intrigued the intellectually curious teenager. He asked his friends who this thirty-something man was, and they told him he was a poet who had grown up in the town and that Gazi should stay away from him, because he had just gotten out of the gulag after serving a ten-year sentence.

"No one would socialize with him, because everybody was afraid they could be arrested or at least harassed," Gazi says. "I became curious to know this person, and I had the courage to approach him and talk to him. This poet, as it turned out, was the well-known Albanian writer Visar Zhiti. He became my mentor."

Already a very good student with strong communication skills and an interest in the written word, Gazi learned a lot from the poet and gained inspiration from him. "I think I became a writer because of him," he says. "He deeply influenced me. And I understood that literature is not just entertaining, but it is very much linked to our existential truths, to our lives. He was jailed for writing literature, poems. This became an ideal for me; I also wanted to become a writer. It's such a courageous thing to do." Gazi, who, today, is the author of many published works, including numerous prize-winning plays and novels, such as his *A Short Border Handbook* (which has, to date, been translated into ten languages), pauses, remembering back to that perilous time.

In this "madhouse" of a country, all foreign literature had been banned. "We lived under the brainwashed propaganda of the Communist Party," he says. "This man was like a human bookstore to me, because he knew so many things and had read so many writers."

The poet, nearly twice Gazi's age, also influenced his political views. He provided the teenager vivid descriptions of his life in prison—all of the tribulation but also all of the heroism. Gazi came to understand that the best, most talented people of his nation—and also maybe the most honest and smartest people—were in jail. They were punished by the regime, something he realized was a huge tragedy. "So, naturally, I sided with these people and their ideals—and also because I came from a family that had suffered from the regime," he says. "From then on, I would be on the side of the losers and very suspicious of the winners. I always want to know more about the losers."

After high school, Gazi was told by the regime to go to the northern part of the country to study biochemistry, because he could best serve the government and its planned economy through a career in that field. "The party needed biochemists, not philosophers or writers or artists," he says. "The party figured it was also looking out for me in terms of the job market and wanted me to be able to make a living, because writers can't unless they are already rich. Ironically, the Communist Party was thinking of me in capitalistic terms."

But Gazi had no interest in biochemistry. He turned his attention to other matters, particularly politics. Like so many others of his generation who saw repressive governments falling, he felt that communism was dying. But the party in his country and one or two others were holdouts, clinging to the last vestiges of their totalitarian power. Students organized to rise up against their nation's respective regimes. "I became part of the anti-regime movement," he says. "We organized the rallies, some of which turned very violent, with the police and protesters clashing. In revolutions, many things happen by chance, by accident, and that's how I became a leader of one of these rallies."

Demonstrators were looting and burning buildings, behavior that's typical in many chaotic uprisings, Gazi says, while drawing comparisons to political protests in the United States. At one rally in his hometown, he tried to stop the pillaging and arson, telling his fellow demonstrators that their purpose should be to build a better world and not sow blind chaos and violence. "After this speech, I was cheered and seen as a leader by the crowd," he says. "Sometime after midnight, hours after the rally concluded, the police started raiding the houses of the people and arresting them."

That's when Gazi decided it was best to go into hiding for a few weeks and, when it was clear that the secret police were determined to find him, to take that clandestine truck ride to the border.

Gaining Fame, Receiving Threats to His Life

Although Gazi had planned to stay in Greece for a short time, until it was safe for him to return to his homeland, he settled in and lived there for more than twenty years. During that time, he pursued his studies at highly regarded universities in Athens, earning a bachelor's degree in philosophy and a doctorate degree in political science and history, writing his PhD thesis on representations of Greeks and Albanians toward each other in Greece.

While Gazi continued his life in academics as an instructor of the history and culture of his homeland, his writing career took off. He gained a loyal audience for the many articles and editorials that he wrote for the largest leftist newspaper in the country and for newspapers in his native country. In addition to journalism, he also wrote several books, including the best-selling and critically acclaimed *A Short Border Handbook*, authored scripts for plays that were staged in prominent theaters, collaborated on a popular video project, and is the recipient of numerous awards by prestigious organizations around the world. Simply put, he became and still is famous in Europe.

But Gazi also gained notoriety within the government and right-wing political groups—primarily because he wrote passionately about the abuse of human rights and the mistreatment of immigrants and refugees, becoming an international advocate for immigrants. Never one to sugarcoat the truth, he often wrote critically of the government and other politically powerful institutions and organizations. He thinks it is for this reason the authorities never processed his application for citizenship, despite all of his many accomplishments and contributions. Even worse, he recounts how, for years, the police, secret police, and the nation's most hyperaggressive, vindictive, white nationalist organization tracked, harassed, and threatened him. When a neo-Nazi party won enough votes to serve in the parliament, the harassment intensified, even becoming life threatening.

"During my time in [that country], I had what I call a schizophrenic existence," Gazi says. "On one hand, I became very well known as a journalist and writer and had and still have a very faithful audience. On the other hand, I became a target for murder."

In 2011, with violence running rampant at the hands of far-right-wing white nationalists, the threats manifested in the form of a physical assault. During a book presentation at the Agios Panteleimon, a well-known public square in Athens, which had become a stronghold of Greece's neo-Nazi party, the Golden Dawn, Gazi was attacked by a group of neo-Nazis and might have been beaten to death had the organizers of the literary event not rescued him. The next day, he went to the authorities to report the attack, but they responded with indifference and even hostility. Shockingly, when Gazi sat down with the city council to tell them what had happened and warn them about the dangerous rise of violent neo-Nazis in Athens, they seemed indifferent to the situation. In fact, the most senior city official present at the meeting fell asleep in the middle of the discussion. While he wasn't completely surprised by their reaction, he was, of course, upset. "It was painful," he says simply.

He made a difficult decision—leave this place he called home. It was clear his life depended on it.

With the situation in that country growing more chaotic and the right-wing extremists gaining power and terrorizing the nation, Gazi got a fortunate break. He was offered and accepted a fellowship at Harvard University, which included a temporary visa. He went on from there to land a teaching position at Emerson College in Boston, had other success in the States, and seriously contemplated taking a big step: applying for a green card and making America his new home.

Taking a Strategic Legal Approach

I met Gazi in September 2013, after he'd been here on a temporary visa for about a year and a half. He initially came to me as a new client for whom we were going to file an asylum status application, because his life clearly would have been in danger if he had to go back to the country where he spent so many years of his life before he had to flee for his safety. The more we talked, the more I appreciated his intelligence, charm, wit, humility, morality, and inner strength. And yet he also carried deep within him an intense fear and an incredible burden of insecurity because of the abuse and mistreatment he suffered by people at the highest levels of the government—all because he speaks out on behalf of immigrants. He was considered a threat to the country because he took a stand for human rights; he'd heard that the authorities had planned to label him "a threat to the public order and national security of the country."

During our initial conversation, I learned more about his background and his many amazing accomplishments as a well-known intellectual, an accomplished and highly regarded writer, playwright, poet, columnist, and advocate for immigrants. But despite his literary and journalistic success, he was viewed as a threat to the country by xenophobic members of Greek society because he was very public in calling for an end to discrimination against immigrants. He shared with me that from 2003 until the day he left Greece to come to Harvard, he was harassed by secret police agents during book presentations or readings. As our conversation began to come to a close for the day, I said to him, "Gazi, we could file for asylum, and I think we'd have a very strong case, but because of your body of work and accomplishments, you might well have a faster, more direct route for a green card on the basis of your extraordinary ability as a writer, and I do a lot of those cases, so I know them when I see them."

I'll never forget Gazi's reaction to my suggestion. His eyes widened and he said, "Extraordinary ability?" He paused and then finished his thought, "Me?" You don't often meet people as accomplished as he is who are also genuinely modest.

"Yes, you," I told him. "We are honored to have people like you in America."

A few years later, Gazi recalls this exchange. "I had never heard that before," he says. "I felt comforted and insulated. I remember saying, 'Maybe it's not possible to get the green card, but I want to thank you so much for saying that. You can't understand how much it means to me.' I had lived in an environment where, as an immigrant, I'd never been told that. It's not a culture that encourages you. They discourage you at every turn—not all the people, but it is predominantly a culture that belittles immigrants. Essentially, they expect immigrants to be grateful to them no matter what. When I heard Susan say she appreciated my accomplishments and liked my book *A Short Border Handbook*, that was a turning point for me. I realized then that I'd made a good decision to live in this country."

At that time, Gazi had another decision to make, about which of course I would thoughtfully and thoroughly advise him: What's the best course of action to attain a green card? When you file for asylum, the person undergoing the asylum case suffers a lot of retraumatization while reviewing over and over again all of the horrific things that happened to him or her. If you can avoid that, it's really for the best emotionally for that person, so when I know I have another way that I feel confident about, I always suggest it as an alternative route to the end goal.

Still, the decision warranted careful consideration of all the pros and cons. It took a long time and a lot of energy to make the best strategic calculation about which way to proceed: filing for asylum or an extraordinary ability status or choosing another route. Throughout that process, I kept thinking about how much was at stake. If whichever avenue we chose didn't work, we were going to have to scramble to find something else to keep him in the States, because he couldn't go back. There were death threats against him.

We ended up filing on the basis of extraordinary ability. In collaboration with Gazi, my team and I put together a lengthy and thick application package. It took almost six months of painstaking preparation while he remained in the same temporary status with his anxiety growing with each passing day—even after the immigrant petition was approved, which is the first of two steps. (Sometimes green cards require three steps.) Then you have to apply for permanent residency. There are a lot of difficult questions on that application, and a misstep in answering any one of those questions could disqualify someone.

Because of this and all that he'd been through, Gazi experienced a tremendous amount of angst. In many ways, he felt everything the archetypal immigrant feels: uncertainty, insecurity, fear, the sense of always looking over your shoulder. He represents the embodiment of the immigrant psyche. The fear of losing a place to live can do someone in. It's so powerful. I would say to him, "Don't worry. I won't let anything happen to you. Please don't worry. I will take care of you." I had to tell him that over and over again, despite his inherent inner strength.

Anyway, the application took a long time to put together, because I wanted it to be perfect to ensure it would work and that he'd be safe and continue making his literary and academic contributions here in the United States as a lawful permanent resident, and later, as an American citizen. And, to our delight, very soon after we filed his extraordinary ability petition, it got approved without any questions.

Journey of Knowing One's Self

Gazi was once asked by a journalist if he considered himself a "citizen of the world." He replied, "I rather consider myself an immigrant of the world. Not only because I'm again an immigrant but also because I want to make a political statement and choice; immigrants today are often viewed the way Jews and the ethnic minorities were viewed in Europe in the '30s. Hatred against the Others, on behalf always of love and protection of the Self, is becoming globally trendy, again. That's why I am and I will always be an immigrant of the world, armed with a temporary residence permit for this earth, incurably intransient."

Yet he's also extremely grateful to live securely as an approved American immigrant, which to some degree he considers his third life. "I feel sometimes that I have lived three lives," he says. "Immigration is never easy, and I feel very fortunate to be here in America. I think the most important thing that America has given me is a much more pluralistic view of life and society. I feel that the American journey has provided me with a lot of self-knowledge about who I am and what I want to do. I would say that the greatest asset of this country is the freedom to search yourself for who you are. In America, I have that freedom."

While he continues to teach and write, he also says he will always work to advance the interests and human rights of immigrants in every society. He also encourages their narratives to be told, because their lives teach us all a lot about ourselves and each other. "I don't know of any country where immigrants haven't contributed to make society better," he says. "It's a dramatic choice of starting from scratch. It requires a determination of will that becomes a second nature to most immigrants. That choice of starting from scratch sparks so much creativity. The best way of understanding the complexities and benefits of immigration is to share our stories and learn about others' stories."

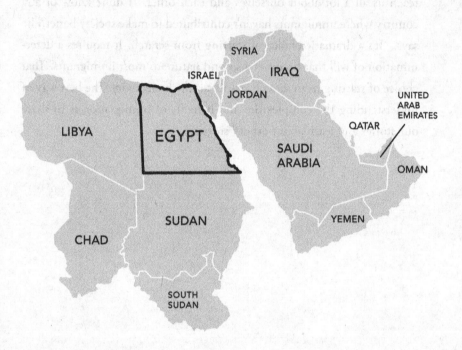

CHAPTER 2

FUSING EQ WITH A.I.:

EGYPTIAN-AMERICAN COMPUTER SCIENTIST AND ENTREPRENEUR PIONEERS TECHNOLOGY TO ENRICH LIVES

Rana el Kaliouby is on a roll—a years-long streak of success that shows no sign of waning. And, when she wins, humanity wins as well. But her victories came only after a lot of anxiety during her immigration process, including a late-night, confrontational encounter at an airport.

Born and raised in Egypt, Rana attended The American University in Cairo, graduating at the top of her class with a degree in computer science. She went on to earn a PhD in this discipline from one of the most prestigious universities on the planet and then worked as a research scientist at a world-class laboratory. But these accomplishments only serve as the foundation for what she has achieved and continues to achieve.

Rana is the cofounder of Affectiva, a cutting-edge, high-tech company in Boston that was recently acquired by Smart Eye, a half-billion-dollar artificial intelligence powerhouse. She now serves as the deputy

CEO of Smart Eye. Rana has often been described as a rock star in her field, particularly for her work in emotion-recognition artificial intelligence that helps people with autism and mental health issues. Already a high-tech icon, critically acclaimed author, public speaker, guest host of a PBS television program about science, and a recipient of numerous awards in business and science, including high honors from both *Forbes* and *Fortune* magazines, Rana has pioneered technology that's changing our lives, and she's only in her early 40s. Oh yes, she's also a devoted single mother of a daughter and a son—and an immigrant.

As smart and successful as she is, Rana also shatters the stereotype of the shy, socially awkward, sometimes condescending computer geek. People are naturally drawn to her because of her warmth, wit, inclusivity, humility, and social grace. And you can't miss the passion in her voice when she talks about her calling in life.

"My entire career," she says when asked about her work, "has been about this mission to bring emotional intelligence and empathy to our devices and our software. The reason why I think this is important is because when I look at human intelligence, I see that the people who are most likable, persuasive, and effective in their jobs, their families, and their personal lives are the ones who have high EQs, emotional IQs."

Rana says these people can read others very well and tap into their emotional intelligence. "You need to clue into people's emotional and mental states and then be able to act accordingly," she says. "That's such a key skill in our life, and I believe it's true for technology as well. As artificial intelligence and technology become more ubiquitous and part of our day-to-day lives, these devices need to understand humans, not only because of the human–machine interaction but also because of the human-to-human communication."

After all, most of our communication now is digital, and if the digital universe is devoid of emotions, she explains, then our EQ levels drop to zero, resulting in an uncompassionate, polarized, cruel digital world. And to a large extent, she says, "That's where we are today. So my team and I are trying to fix that."

This is no doubt a lofty but worthy goal, and one she'll likely achieve. In fact, she and her colleagues at her company have made great strides as there are already many practical applications of this groundbreaking technology for which she's led the way, with more on the horizon.

Sobbing Buckets of Tears at a Customs Checkpoint

I first met Rana in 2009 when she contacted me by phone after one of her mentors at MIT (and a former client of mine) recommended that she get her visa situation in better shape and referred her to me. Naturally, I was very impressed with her and her career and business plans. I knew immediately that I wanted to help her. Years later, Rana remembered that initial phone conversation, and I include her recollection here because I think it helps demonstrate her modesty.

"I spoke with Susan on the phone," Rana recalls in talking with a friend, "and, at the time, I was just this random Egyptian postgrad. I pitched her my ideas and my plans for the company—I'm sure she gets hundreds of these calls all the time—but, for some reason, she bought into it and said, 'Okay, let's do it.'"

In the fall of 2009, I helped Rana apply for and receive an O-1 temporary work visa, which gave her the right to stay for several years. The O-1 visa is also known as an *extraordinary ability* visa (sometimes called the *Einstein visa*) because it is available only to the crème de la crème—those who have reached the very tops of their fields.

Then, in early 2010, we filed an extraordinary ability immigrant petition, so she would be able to settle in the U.S. permanently. For both of these, Rana had to gather evidence, and, for the most part and from my point of view, her entire immigration process was fairly straightforward— more like simple arithmetic than complex calculus. We ran into very few obstacles, primarily because the value she'd bring to this country was evident; she's easily one of the smartest people I've ever met. Put another way, she obviously possesses extraordinary ability.

Now, that doesn't mean she didn't feel pressure and even feel overwhelmed at times. Like most of my clients, she did, because satisfying the immigration requirements can be very taxing. Or, as she puts it, "It seemed like there were a bazillion hoops to get through. I couldn't believe the sheer amount of material that was needed."

The evidence required for an O-1 visa includes letters of recommendation, which, for Rana, meant asking for referrals from professors at the universities she attended, her advisor during her journey to earn a PhD, the director of the lab where she worked, and several others. That was relatively easy, but she felt uncomfortable with another requirement.

"I had to get letters of recommendation from people who I'd never worked with but who are experts in my field," she recalls. "So I had to reach out to all these people and say, 'Hey, you don't know me, but can you write me a letter of recommendation that speaks to the quality and unique nature of my work?'"

Rana also had to demonstrate her public presence. "I guess because we had to make the case that I'm extraordinary or whatever, we had to compile all of the press coverage and the publications that I was in," she says. "This was in 2009 and 2010, when I was a fairly young researcher in this space. It would be quite different if I had to do that today, because now I have a few more accolades."

That's quite an understatement. Conduct a Google search of Rana, and you'll see a very long list of search engine hits of her name, life, career accomplishments, photos of her, awards she's won, articles she's written, articles written about her, reviews of her book, podcasts, TED Talk speeches, YouTube videos, and on and on.

Nonetheless, the process moved forward fairly smoothly. Rana did, however, experience a scary late-night encounter with an immigration official at a major international airport here in the United States.

During this time, she was commuting back and forth between Egypt and the United States, because the man who's now her ex-husband and is the father of her children was based in Cairo and her kids went to school there. One time, in late 2009, she was traveling with her baby son Adam, and after they exited the plane, exhausted and eager to get home, they attempted to pass through customs. Adam was born here in the United States, so he's American, and she was reentering the country with her Egyptian passport. The immigration official stopped her and—although he was mistaken in his assessment—told her there was a problem with her visa.

She recounts that experience: "The immigration guy said, 'You're denied entry, but your son can go in.' I said, 'Well, my son is about six months old. So we'll just take a flight back to Egypt, and then we'll sort this out.' The guy said, 'No, your son can't leave the United States now that he's landed.' They took us into this room in the airport. Adam is, of course, hungry and crying, and I'm sobbing. And I asked to make one phone call. It was about eleven o'clock at night. I called Susan, and I was sobbing to her, tears streaming down my face. She spoke to the guy and did her magic."

Ethics, Diversity, and Leadership

Over the next several years, we took all the steps necessary to help Rana become a naturalized U.S. citizen, receiving the Certificate of Naturalization in early 2016. She is now officially an Egyptian-American contributor to our society—and what a contributor she is indeed. She and her company have created an area of artificial intelligence that didn't even exist a few short years ago. It's a powerful force for change, and Rana speaks about it proudly.

"My team and I painted this vision of the world that has emotion-enabled technology, and we pushed it out there," she says. "People got on board and are excited about it. We have investors, we have competition, and I feel like we've created this ecosystem."

For four years and counting, her company has held an artificial intelligence summit, an annual industry event that brings people together around this new vision of human-centric AI. And with Rana at the helm, her company has earned recognition for doing things the right way. "We have very strong core values," she says, "and we advocate for ethics, which, I think, is unusual for a small start-up like us to prioritize the ethical and moral implications of the technology in building a productive ecosystem."

In addition to creating innovative technology, managing the nuts and bolts of her business, and contributing to the greater good of society, Rana takes a lot of pride in the diverse team she has assembled around her—something she talks about in various speaking engagements. While the majority of her U.S. employees are Americans, a number of her colleagues and team members are like her, in that they weren't born and raised in the United States but came here to pursue and earn their master's degrees or their PhDs. Rana recruited them, and I have had the honor of helping many of them secure their immigration status.

"We have a Canadian scientist who runs our science team," Rana says. "He and his wife came to the U.S., and they now have green cards. They bought a house here and have two kids who are American. There's another team member who's Indian and another who's Persian. We're such an international team. [The company] and I are playing a part in these people's professional journeys but, more importantly, their personal journeys as well. I've attended their weddings, I know their kids, and I'm proud of that. It essentially started with Susan saying to me, 'Yeah, I'll do your O-1.' It's part of a ripple effect of all these people who may not have stayed in this country. I feel good about that."

Rana's involvement in her teammates' personal journeys fits squarely within the leadership model she employs as the CEO—as do empathy, integrity, and ethics. "I'm a very core-values-driven leader," she says, adding that the company's values aren't merely marketing fluff to stick on the website or espouse at public appearances. "We turn down business that we feel is not aligned with our core values; if it's not ethical and not moral, we reject it. I lead with the same set of core values that I use to parent my kids: Work hard, get stuff done, and prioritize the human connection."

This approach extends beyond the walls of the business, as she and her team members also take a personal interest in their external partners, like investors. "There's a human element with them as well," she says. "I know the families of my investors. I take a human interest in them personally."

What's more, Rana's not afraid to show her vulnerabilities, something that many leaders never do, which is a mistake, according to Dudley Slater, a former CEO of a major telecom company and a coauthor of *Fusion Leadership: Unleashing the Movement of Monday Morning Enthusiasts.* Slater says Fusion Leaders—as he calls those who follow this leadership model—are often most effective when they're "demonstrating candor and exhibiting vulnerability," he writes in his book. By doing so, they can help all of the members of an organization strive and achieve collective goals. "True leadership shows people how to connect and commit to a common cause and helps them understand how they're part of something bigger than themselves."

Clearly, Rana understands the value of "demonstrating candor and exhibiting vulnerability." One manifestation of this comes through very clearly in an article she wrote for a popular and highly regarded business magazine, one of her many publications. In it, she talks openly about her divorce and the challenges of being a single mother. She candidly describes for all to see the deterioration of her marriage, the pressures both she and her ex-husband felt in trying to make it work, and the difficulties of essentially living simultaneously on two distant continents and regularly commuting between them.

She believes that, ultimately, she gained a lot of strength in admitting her marriage was failing and deciding that divorce was best for both her and her ex-husband. "That's when I became a misfit, and the voice of doubt in my head got louder," she writes in the article. "For years, I was my own worst critic. It's taken a divorce, a cross-continental move, and a lot of missteps to learn to coexist with the voice in my head and to turn it into an empowering force."

Those thoughts and the other related ones she expresses in the article really resonated with people. "I was just floored by the number of people, both women and men, who directly messaged me to say how much they could relate to what I went through and the feelings I had," she says, adding that she built a connection with these people even though she's never met them in person. She also acknowledges that writing the piece, laying it all out on the line, was cathartic. But, again, it's the act of demonstrating vulnerability and candor that's important.

"I've found that being vulnerable and open builds so much good will, trust, and reciprocity," Rana says and recounts the content of an email she wrote to her coworkers in the spring of 2020, at the height of the COVID-19 pandemic. She and other company leaders crafted policies on working remotely and other guidelines for team members to follow and sent them out in a company-wide email. But then she wrote a second, more personal message that demonstrated her own fears and concerns.

"I just wanted to follow up with a human message," she says. "I said, 'This is a terrible situation for everybody. Like so many of you, my kids are going to learn from home, whatever that means. So I'm confronted with all this news all the time, and it's draining, but we're going to have to pull together. We can give up, or we can pull together and make this work.' I thought I needed to rally the troops and be a leader. I ended it with saying something like 'Okay, please share your tips about working from home and dealing with what we're going through.' The response was amazing."

Rana's book *Girl Decoded*, which was released in 2020, is another powerful example of Rana's willingness to put herself out there and demonstrate her humanity and vulnerability. In this riveting memoir, she chronicles her evolution from a "nice Egyptian girl" growing up in a traditional environment in the Middle East to a revolutionary, path-breaking scientist, start-up founder, and world renowned business leader. Her book brims with emotional honesty and candor.

Grateful and "Serving as the Bridge"

Rana is anything but reticent in expressing her gratitude about living in this country, saying that her citizenship is a privilege that also comes with a great deal of responsibility. While she says she "loves" being an American, she also embraces her heritage as an Egyptian, which she feels constitutes an equally important part of her identity. "I love both, and I'm proud of both," she says. "I feel very lucky to be here, to make this country my home, and to see my kids grow up here and realize the ample opportunities all around them. It's special for me as an Egyptian woman to come here and start a company, breaking the mold in so many ways, and be celebrated. I'm grateful for that."

Yet, as much as Rana loves this country and cherishes the opportunities available here in the United States to build a business, succeed financially, create jobs, raise her family, and break new technological ground in meaningful ways that enhance people's lives and transform the world, she's not blind to the nation's problems, and sometimes, they affect her family personally. Rana sponsored her parents for U.S. green cards so they could spend more time together as a family, and as a result of the COVID-19 travel ban imposed by former President Trump, their immigrant visa applications (along with everyone else's) were put on hold—delaying their arrival in the U.S. by nearly eighteen months. It was not until President Biden took office that her parents were finally approved for permanent residence status, and happily, now the family has been reunited.

When, in the earliest days of his presidency, Donald Trump issued his infamous Muslim travel ban, she was, of course, deeply disturbed, as many of us were. But, for her, it was a personal attack.

"It was awful—and not just because of the treatment but also because of the ramifications," says Rana, a practicing Muslim. "I felt that, unfortunately, he was giving permission to people to hate on Muslims. I also felt it was so unfounded. At the core of Islam are love, generosity, compassion, and kindness. I believed it ran counter to the spirit of this country, which is what we're trying to replicate in our own little way at our company, this open-mindedness and bringing diverse people in because they have different ways of seeing the world. How awesome is that? And he was defiling that."

I like that Rana points out the central tenets of Islam, with love as the core. Many people don't hear that enough or even at all. We need to be exposed to more examples of that and fewer examples of, as she says, "the stereotypical stuff that Trump was riffing off of."

She feels that, to some extent, she and her kids can, from their life in a Northeast suburb, help change perceptions and paint a different portrait of the Muslim community. Her daughter and son attend a prep school where many students and teachers have not interacted with people from the Middle East. "So I feel that we're ambassadors," she says. "Both of my kids take that very seriously. They talk a lot about what it's like to grow up in the Middle East and the family traditions we have. We often open our house and host other people, because we want to share. In a way, we've integrated the two cultures. I feel that we play an important role by serving as the bridge."

CHAPTER 3

GAINING KNOWLEDGE, GROWING WEALTH, GIVING BACK:

SOMALI IMMIGRANT WINS POLITICAL ASYLUM CASE, CONTRIBUTES GLOBALLY

In 2018, Jamal Ali Hussein was riding in a car with two other men in his East African homeland of Somaliland (the northern section of Somalia, which has its own independent government). They were traveling to a meeting in the central part of a large city. He looked out the window, saw a teenage boy hitchhiking along the road, thought for a moment, and asked the man driving the car and the other passenger if they could stop. "I think we should give this young man a ride," Jamal recalls saying.

The teen jogged up to where the vehicle had stopped, got in, and thanked the men. The driver asked him where he was going and where he had come from. The boy said he was heading into the central city and was coming from home. "And where is home, young man?" the driver asked.

The boy replied, "I live in the city Burco, in the village of Ali Hussein."

Knowing that the nearby village was named after Jamal's father, a former well-respected government official and high-ranking military officer in the nation's armed services, the driver glanced at Jamal, looked at the other man, grinned, and asked the boy, "Do you go to school?"

"Yes, I go to the Ali Hussein Primary and Intermediate School," he replied.

The driver pointed at Jamal and asked the teenager another question: "Do you know who this man is?"

"Yes, of course I know," he said. "I saw him on TV, and he's the man who built our school." Jamal smiled to himself, turned to the young student, and smiled at him.

Jamal had indeed financed the construction of the school with money out of his own pocket and felt grateful that he could contribute to the village. The school opened ten years earlier, in 2008, replacing a small, two-room building. At the time, Jamal served as a senior international executive and business leader for a large multinational bank, a financial institution that has earned a reputation for its generous community service in the markets in which it operates. One day, he received a call from someone with ties to the village who mentioned the inadequate school and asked Jamal if he could help in some way.

"The next time I traveled back to my birthplace, I made a special trip to the village, conducted an assessment of the school, and asked to meet with the village elders," Jamal recalls. "During the meeting, I asked them, 'What can I do for you? How can I contribute?'"

The elders didn't hesitate in answering Jamal: "One of them said, 'My friend, can you help us build a real school? We have so many children, and the students take turns learning from their teachers in the two-room building.' They told me that the students have shifts during the school day. One shift starts early in the morning and finishes at around 11:00, and then another group of students comes in and finishes around 3:00, and then another group comes in. The village is so poor, and that's how they used to run this school."

The international bank where Jamal worked finances many worthy projects around the world, in keeping with its commitment to community service and often at Jamal's behest during his tenure there. But his home country didn't qualify for receiving financial backing for this school, because it was outside of the bank's sphere of operation. "Besides that, I did not want it to appear as a conflict of interest since my family was involved," he says. So he financed the project with his own money, approached one of the nation's largest construction companies, told them what type of design he wanted for the school building, and awarded them the work contract.

The local municipality decided to name the school after Jamal's father in remembrance of his bravery and his dedication to his country. After the contractor completed construction, Jamal ran the school for the first six months and personally paid the teachers' and staff members' salaries while also picking up the tab for various other expenses. Toward the end of that six-month period, he met with the nation's minister of education and other government officials. "I said, 'Guys, the village is growing, and I can't handle running this school myself anymore. You need to take over.' They came to see the school, made an assessment, took control of it, and began paying the teacher salaries and covering other costs."

Although Jamal is a modest man, you can hear the pride in his voice when he talks about the Ali Hussein Primary and Intermediate School and all the children who have benefited from its teachers' instruction. "According to my last count, more than 2,000 students have attended the school," he says. "I'm so grateful the village elders asked me for assistance."

He's also grateful that he had the financial means to make such an important contribution. While he's always had the heart to help, it was his hard work, intelligence, and an assist years earlier from an unlikely arm of the U.S. government—against all odds—that laid the foundation that enabled him to build the much-needed school.

Clearly, Jamal has come a long way since living much of his childhood as a nomad, herding goats and sheep in a remote African desert. As a young man, he immigrated to the United States and became an American citizen. He earned an MBA from Harvard and embarked on a successful career as a highly respected, award-winning businessman who has traveled the globe handling complex, high-finance matters and managing teams of sophisticated employees while orchestrating life-enhancing community service projects in dozens of places in dire need. His story is one of perseverance and compassion.

From Nomad to Table Tennis Champ to U.S. Visitor

Jamal and his brother and sisters grew up in a home with loving, supportive parents who placed an emphasis on education and hard work; they considered knowledge the greatest form of wealth. He lived in the city with his family during the school year, but his grandfather wanted him to "experience the nomadic life so that I did not forget how my forefathers lived, and the way at least more than half the people [in his home country] still live, moving their families several times a year, based on the seasons and the rainfalls," he writes in his book in progress about his life's journey.

Consequently, he spent his summers as a herdsman, caring for sheep and goats, eating one primary meal a day, which consisted of rice and milk, and sleeping outside on the desert floor.

"My grandfather wanted me to know this way of life, and he thought it would toughen me for life and, in a way, he was right," Jamal writes. "Those solitary days with the goats made me understand and trust myself. They gave me a connection to the land. At night, I slept on the ground outside the hut with the other men and boys; the women and children usually slept inside the hut. But being a nomad also sparked in me the desire to get as far away from a sustenance life as I could."

To avoid a future as a nomad, Jamal studied very hard in school and achieved significant academic success, always finishing the school year at or near the top of his class. He also succeeded with a ping-pong paddle in his hand, competing in many table tennis tournaments across the country and winning National Table Tennis Championships three years in a row. His exploits earned him media coverage in newspapers and on the radio. He fantasized that his fame would enable him to cross the Atlantic Ocean, land on the shores of the United States, and live there.

After high school, he attended one of the best universities in his nation and graduated with a BS degree in accounting and management. He learned how to read and speak English by spending time in the lobby of the American embassy in Somaliland's largest city, where he'd read *The New York Times*, *The Washington Post*, *Newsweek*, and *Time* and watch CNN, ABC News, CBS's *60 Minutes*, and other American TV programs.

During his university education, Jamal would give regular updates on his academic progress to his family, including his uncle in the United States. Uncle Bulhan had taught at a prominent East Coast university and ran a very successful and profitable health management company in Boston. Those performance reports were glowing, as Jamal consistently received A grades, motivated in part by Uncle Bulhan's promise that, if his nephew did well in college, he'd bring him to America and have him stay with his family. And sure enough, he lived up to his vow. The plan was for Jamal to visit the States, experience all this country had to offer, look at and consider graduate schools, go back to his home country, get a proper student visa, and return to the United States.

But that plan hit an obstacle when Jamal first arrived on American soil in September 1989—with only $64 in his pocket. He was detained for hours by an overzealous immigration agent at Boston's Logan Airport who questioned the young East African harshly. The officer saw that Jamal was carrying his bachelor's diploma and transcripts, and he didn't believe Jamal when he told the officer he was only planning to visit relatives in Boston for a few months, look into graduate schools, and go back home to apply for a student visa. The officer suspected Jamal wanted to stay permanently in the U.S., and he expressed doubt that Jamal's relatives, who'd be picking him up, had the financial means to house and feed him.

The agent intended to deny him entry and send him back across the Atlantic. But, ultimately, Jamal was able to use a combination of his beguiling charisma, earnest countenance, and persuasive speaking skills to convince the agent to allow him into the country—but with very strict conditions attached: The agent kept Jamal's passport, his educational documents and transcripts, and his personal effects and told Jamal that he'd need to present himself for further proceedings to prove he truly had a right to stay.

Jamal was lucky. The nation's immigration law presumes that everyone coming to the United States has *immigrant intent*, and it's up to each person seeking entry to the U.S. to prove otherwise. Around the world each year, U.S. consular officers deny hundreds of thousands of visitor visa applications to would-be visitors. And U.S. Customs officers at our airports and borders often deny admission to people seeking to enter the States as visitors, even though many truly intend only to visit.

Soon after the encounter at the airport, Jamal moved into his cousin's house and would often spend his days in the library, reading about a variety of topics and the daily news, including disturbing reports regarding his native country and the murder and brutality inflicted by the dictatorial government against its own citizens. Of course, he'd known about the tyranny for a long time, but after he arrived in the U.S., the conditions grew worse. He worried about his family. He especially worried about his father.

Then, in October, several weeks after his arrival in New England, he received an upsetting letter from his father, who wrote that he had quit his government position, defected from the military, and fled to Ethiopia. The rest of his family had also escaped Somalia, and many family members were living in one of the many refugee camps that sheltered the two million people who had escaped the violent wrath of the dictatorship. His father told his son in that letter that he should by no means return to his homeland. His life would be at great risk. Jamal was shaken, but knew he must find a way to stay in the United States.

With his time to legally stay in the States running out and an imminent court date to prove his initial entry was for a valid purpose, he sought help.

Meeting Jamal

I met Jamal in the autumn of 1989, when I was a young associate at my law firm, after we were connected by a nonprofit organization called the Political Asylum/Immigration Representation Project (PAIR), which I have been actively involved with since its inception in 1989 and which I'm proud to serve as the president of its board. PAIR provides bona fide asylum-seekers who can't afford legal counsel with local lawyers who take their cases on a pro bono basis.

At the time, PAIR was so new that Jamal was the group's first client. He came to my office at Mintz seeking legal representation in applying for political asylum. I asked him to tell me his story, and he talked and talked—all morning long. He had also laid out his case for asylum on paper, in a narrative that was very detailed and quite well written. I was impressed by the articulate way he presented himself and by his obvious intelligence and earnestness.

The more I learned about his father, the more I wanted to help. His father served as one of the highest-ranking officers in the Somali military and had to work closely with the president. That is, until that leader turned into a deranged tyrant and began ordering his troops to systematically round up members of opposition tribes, mow them down with machine guns, and toss their bodies into mass graves.

Jamal's father and other key military officers knew they had to get out. They defected, agreed to join the forces fighting to overthrow the president, and left the country in a dangerous and harrowing escape that took them through the desert for several days until they reached Ethiopia, the staging ground for the rebel movement. His father served as the highest-ranking military officer to defect, and as a brilliant military strategist, his leadership and support of the rebel forces was instrumental to their success (and, ultimately, in overthrowing the corrupt government). The president saw this as the ultimate act of betrayal, and it enraged him. He declared the men to be traitors and issued an order for them to be captured and executed. That rage of retaliation extended to the families of the defectors; the president and his henchmen had already murdered countless family members of those who opposed the regime.

It became clear to me that, if Jamal was denied asylum and sent back to his country, his life would be in jeopardy. To be blunt: Deportation would essentially serve as his death warrant.

To say the least, his story was a lot for me to absorb. We needed to take a lunch break. I asked him what he'd like to eat, and he didn't know what to order from our local deli, which is understandable, given that he'd not been in the United States for long and had only once gone to an American grocery store to get a few things for him and his cousin. He had returned from his first shopping trip with what he thought was a can of tuna fish. It was actually . . . cat food. (He and his cousin had a good laugh.) So I ordered for him—his first-ever turkey sandwich, which he loved and devoured. After lunch, we got back to work and, by the end of the day, I knew I was about to take on my first political asylum case.

As our meeting came to a close, I told Jamal that my team and I would do everything we could to help him apply for asylum status. He looked me in the eyes and flashed that infectious smile that I would see time and time again over the coming months and, as it turned out, over the next thirty-plus years. He was so visibly relieved. But I cautioned him: It would be difficult to succeed, asylum-seekers face tough odds, he must be patient, and we'd have to work diligently together to build the best case possible.

I also told him I was committed to winning the case and gaining him the political asylum he deserved. Jamal thanked me profusely and told me he would entrust his case to me. I could actually see the relief in his face as he left my office that day.

Assembling an Airtight Argument for Asylum

After I saw Jamal out, I walked back to my office in a bit of a daze. I stared out of my fortieth-floor window and scanned the Boston skyline, feeling a confluence of emotions sweep through me. First, I experienced a burst of adrenaline as I realized this case represented the precise reason I wanted to be an immigration lawyer in the first place—to help people like my new client. So, I was excited. But I also felt a heavy weight pressing down on my shoulders, because, by agreeing to take Jamal's case, I had essentially placed this man's life in my hands. His fate rested on my legal acumen, my ability to build an airtight argument for asylum. Was I up to this daunting task?

At the same time, I knew that if ever a human being deserved sanctuary in the United States, it was this bright, warm, compassionate young man. What he told me was so powerful that I felt confident I could prove the life-threatening danger he would face if he were deported and make the case that it's incumbent upon the U.S. government to safeguard Jamal. I felt fiercely protective of him, a feeling I have about all my clients who face life-altering consequences if their cases fail.

Fairly early on after meeting Jamal, after representing him in the hearing to prove he had always had a lawful purpose in seeking to enter our country, I secured a work authorization card for him, enabling him to obtain gainful employment. Soon thereafter, he interviewed for a job at a local bank. He was chosen from scores of other applicants, a testament to his prowess in accounting and other bank-related business, as well as his winning personality. He enjoyed his position, coworkers, and work environment, but the threat of deportation loomed over him.

Over several months, my team and I worked with Jamal to gather the necessary letters of support from people who knew him, the documentation of political turmoil in his homeland and the heinous crimes committed by that country's president and his enforcers, and other information that would help us construct a compelling and convincing narrative to the judge who would hear our case.

We assembled documents that, when stacked, stood two feet high. But I wanted something more. I felt we needed a piece of evidence that would clinch the case—indisputable evidence that Jamal's father had served at the highest levels of his government. One day I asked him, "Did your father ever come to the United States on official business on behalf of your country? If we can offer the judge clear-cut evidence that he did, we will prove the importance of his high rank and role in the government and why his defection to join the rebel forces would anger the dictator enough to have him and any or all of your family members executed."

Now at this time, Jamal had no direct contact with his father, who was fighting on the front lines; he couldn't call or write to him, nor did he even know where he was. For the safety of everybody, none of the family could know his whereabouts. But he might be able to reach his father through one of his uncles via a byzantine route of communication, although that wouldn't be quick or easy. This uncle had also joined the rebel forces, and I asked Jamal to reach out to him to find out if his father had visited the United States and, if so, when. Jamal asked him, and his uncle promised he would do his best.

"A few weeks later, I came [home] to find the red light blinking on my phone machine," Jamal writes in his book. "I pressed the button to listen to my messages and heard my uncle's deep voice speaking rapidly. 'I spoke with your dad at the front, and he thinks he led a delegation to the States in the early 1980s. Maybe 1982. That first few months of 1982 is what he remembers.'"

This could be big, I recall thinking at the time, in July 1990. *But only if we can prove it—ideally, in writing.* So I reached out to people I thought could help. One thing about the legal profession that many people may not fully realize is that many law firms cultivate and maintain close working relationships with lawyers within their big firms, as well as across the profession, with lawyers at other firms. I'm fortunate because the network of attorneys within Mintz is tight; we're constantly leaning on each other for help, and that's what I did when Jamal told me that his father led a delegation to the United States, mostly likely to our nation's capital.

Because time was of the essence, I immediately contacted a senior attorney in our Washington, DC, office who had previously served as an assistant secretary of state in the Reagan administration. Although I was only a junior associate at the time, I picked up the phone and asked this colleague I had never met if he could help. To my delight, he agreed to try.

I asked my colleague if he'd contact the Pentagon to see if someone within the Department of Defense could check its visitation records to see if we could verify the meeting Jamal's father had with Defense officials. Within only a few days, we received a letter from a U.S. African regional official within the Defense Department. It stated that Jamal's father was indeed a colonel and the director of communications of his country's government, as well as a member of a military delegation that met with none other than Caspar Weinberger, Reagan's secretary of defense.

I remember looking at that letter in near disbelief and staring at the impressive seal of the Pentagon emblazed on the top of the official Department of Defense stationery. *Yes, this is big*, I thought again.

In that letter, we had incontrovertible evidence that Jamal's father worked closely with the nation's president (before he became a murderous tyrant) and the logical extrapolations that rippled from that fact: He had defected and was most certainly now an enemy of the dictator, who, clearly, would want revenge and would seek it in any way he could, including by killing defectors' family members. Consequently, if he was deported, Jamal's life would be in grave danger.

Of course, Jamal knew the import of receiving this key piece of evidence and has called the day it arrived one of the happiest of his life. I concur; it was for me as well!

All Rise; This Court Is Now in Session

But my team and I still had work to do to prepare our case for a hearing, which had been set for September. Even with the Pentagon letter—the ace in our hand of cards—we needed to get everything in order. The judge hearing our case was known for denying political asylum cases and deporting asylum-seekers, and in fact, it's an uphill battle to win such cases in many venues, considering the subjectivity of those rendering the up or down ruling. In the previous couple of years, only seven of the more than 190 asylum-seekers who appeared before this judge had won their cases. So, it was impossible to overprepare.

My team and I constructed the narrative strategically, taking care to present it convincingly but not melodramatically. In many ways, the powerful facts spoke for themselves, but we had to set the stage just right to let them shine. I prepped Jamal for hours, as he needed to be ready to handle any question the judge might hurl his way. I also told him that, while I thought we'd win, we might not. He had to be prepared for heartbreaking disappointment—and so did I.

I had legal backup waiting in the wings to support our case. I had asked the Washington director of Human Rights Watch to be ready to provide expert testimony via telephone at any time during what was scheduled as a possible four-hour hearing. She was well versed in the political climate of Jamal's war-torn home country and could attest to the dangers he would most certainly encounter if he were forced to return. It was comforting to know she was there for us if we needed her—and I needed all the comfort I could get.

I didn't sleep much the night before the hearing. And I was nervous as I entered the courtroom that day. After all, it's not a reach to say that my client's life was at stake. Jamal was, understandably, downright scared.

As it turns out, we only needed one of the scheduled four hours. The judge had reviewed all of our paperwork and addressed us and the attorneys representing the other side, the U.S. Immigration and Naturalization Service. He said he strongly believed Jamal should be granted asylum. I could hardly believe my ears. Nevertheless, opposing counsel argued against such a ruling, and I hit back with what I thought was a concise but powerful line of reasoning. The judge listened to both sides argue—actually for only a matter of several minutes and without calling Jamal for his testimony. His Honor took it all in, paused, and then stood by his initial inclination, granting Jamal asylum and handing us the victory.

The judge's decision to grant Jamal asylum happened so much more quickly than we were expecting that both Jamal and I initially found ourselves in a state of disbelief, but this quickly gave way to pure elation. Justice had been served, and Jamal no longer had to fear for his very life. Over the next few hours, the sweetness of this victory washed over me. When I went back to my office, I couldn't concentrate on any other work that afternoon.

I lay awake for hours that night, too excited to fall asleep.

Making the Most of the Opportunity

I was convinced at the time, and I still am today, that in all of the hundreds of documents we supplied to the judge, the most pivotal piece of paper came in the form of that letter from the Department of Defense.

I believe that it's very rare in the history of asylum in the United States for someone to receive a letter from the U.S. Pentagon supporting rather than challenging someone's claim to asylum.

Winning asylum allowed Jamal to forge his destiny. He has certainly made the most of his asylum status and achieved great success, including earning an MBA from Harvard Business School. While taking classes in this prestigious master's program, Jamal also accomplished something he could have only dreamed about when he was a child: On March 28, 1996, at the age of 32, he became an American citizen.

One of his Harvard classmates learned about his naturalization process and organized a small celebration on campus. The first day he returned to class after earning his citizenship, Jamal strolled down the hall and heard people chatting louder than usual. When he entered the classroom, he paused and thought he'd walked into the wrong room. He refocused his eyes and scanned the room as the other students fell silent. What he saw stunned him. The classmate who knew about his big day had decorated every desk with red, white, and blue balloons and small American flags.

The professor, one of Jamal's favorites, then spoke up: "Before we start the class, let's celebrate with our student and section mate Jamal Hussein, who became an American citizen last Thursday." The students and the professor then erupted in applause, smiles beaming brightly, emotions running high.

"I was so surprised. I couldn't believe it," Jamal says, years later. "It was such a wonderful gesture, and I was so grateful."

While Jamal had been advancing his career in the financial arena even before his time at Harvard—he had worked several years as a senior associate at a Big Five accounting firm and earned a CPA license—after he left the university with an MBA degree, his career took flight.

He landed a key position at one of America's best-known multinational banks, serving in roles with such titles as regional vice president, corporate finance and capital markets head, director, and managing director. Ultimately, he was promoted to the highest-level jobs in the bank worldwide, serving in various countries around the world as bank country chief and CEO/managing director of the bank's foreign subsidiaries. These positions and others took him to Trinidad and Tobago, Belize, Saudi Arabia, Kenya, Tanzania, and other nations where he conducted a range of high-finance work, managed the bank's employees, and won several highly regarded service awards. Today, he runs his own consulting firm.

Oh yes, in keeping with a long, storied tradition of lyrical appreciation in his home nation, Jamal is also a poet and songwriter. His published poetry and the performances of his songs on YouTube have gained a loyal following.

But if you ask him how he would characterize himself, he'd likely say he's an "international banker with a conscience." As I mentioned earlier, Jamal was a pivotal player in the bank's foundation that supports and funds community service projects around the world, including here in the United States. It is a win–win arrangement, because the bank helps those in need and, in so doing, generates goodwill and positive PR for its efforts. Jamal was not shy about asking the bank to donate to projects he believed needed and deserved financial assistance.

"When you are the CEO of [a nation's branch of a bank] you are the top guy," he says. "We had a fairly large budget, and the executives could request more money and ask [the bank] to give more to a particular community. I was always asking for more money for the communities. We built houses and helped orphanages and hospitals and created and ran mentorship programs for high school and college students. I gained a lot of satisfaction providing financial support and guidance for their careers. We were all over the place and always involved in the community. Sometimes, our staff and I would go to hospitals over the weekend to help the patients."

Jamal stays very active helping his home country, which eventually survived the tyranny of the dictatorial government from which his father defected, as well as subsequent corrupt regimes. (Jamal's father is credited by many as the mastermind behind the military tactic which resulted in the capture of the city of Berbera, in Somalia, on January 23, 1991. The dictator, Siad Barre, fled the country forever three days later, on January 26, 1991.) Jamal was even a popular candidate for the presidency of his homeland, and although he didn't prevail, he continues to support the rebuilding of democracy there.

But if he had to narrow down the accomplishments he's most proud of, he'd point to his marriage to his beloved wife and their four children. "I got the opportunity in the United States to come in and be given a chance to make something out of myself," he says. "I'm happy that my children were born in the U.S., and that they can accomplish anything that they want in this country. That's one of the biggest accomplishments I've achieved."

Jamal's four children have grown up doing the things kids do: They play sports, socialize with friends, go to movies, and listen to music. They also follow in Jamal's footsteps in that they work diligently in school, shine as role models, and achieve excellent academic success. Two attend very well-regarded, academically rigorous U.S. universities, the third youngest just graduated from high school and received a full scholarship to a competitive university, and the remaining high schooler eagerly looks forward to college. All four have their sights set on pursuing professional careers in which they can help others. As is the case with so many children of immigrants, they will no doubt extend the type of goodwill that Jamal has done throughout his life and continues to do.

I'm fortunate to have had a close friendship with Jamal and his family for more than 30 years, and our families have enjoyed many dinners and special occasions together. My family and I even visited them when Jamal served as the president of the bank in Tanzania. We always have fun and know that our families will be there for each other in good times and bad.

I often think about what Jamal told *The Boston Globe* many years ago, when the newspaper published a photo of him that accompanied a feature story about him and others who immigrated to this country, received citizenship, and were making important contributions to our society. "So many countries close their borders," he told the *Globe*. "But all kinds of immigrants come here. They are a pool of talented people who see different things. They see things with fresh eyes."

While Jamal has helped people around the world in his capacity of a conscientious banker, he has also contributed so much to enhance people's lives here in the United States—without expecting or wanting any fanfare. He's led extensive academic and career mentoring programs that have helped young people who are immigrants or are simply struggling to succeed in this country. He also donates large sums to many worthy causes in his community and across the nation. Again, he does this quietly and won't talk about these contributions unless asked.

None of this would have happened had Jamal not won asylum. If he'd been deported, he'd have surely been incarcerated, tortured, and killed. Instead, he has gone on to demonstrate his appreciation and compassion and enrich the lives of Americans—something he vowed to do if he were allowed to stay and live in the United States. "So many people have helped me in my life," he says, "and, when the judge granted me asylum, I promised myself that I'd do all I could to give back."

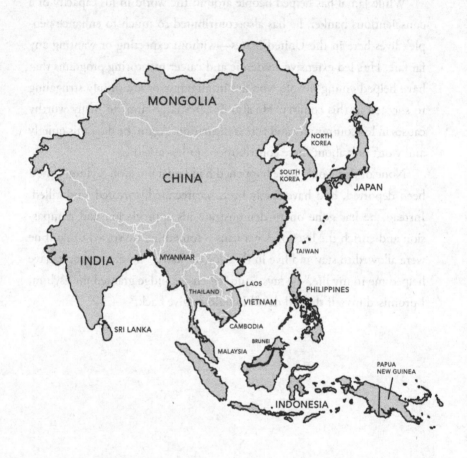

CHAPTER 4

HITTING ALL THE RIGHT NOTES:

ASIAN-BORN VIRTUOSO VIOLINIST
MAKES AMERICA PROUD

A lot of people, perhaps too many, crowd into my law firm's largest conference room with its floor-to-ceiling views of the Boston Harbor. We have no compulsion to go outside and enjoy the sunny, sixty-nine-degree weather on this bright, warm afternoon in mid-April 2009. Elated to be packed together indoors, we stand in celebration and anticipation. All the eyes, ears, and attention of my fellow Mintz Levin lawyers, staff members, and our guests are focused on a twelve-year-old Asian-born girl.

Wearing a simple but beautiful dress, her long black hair pulled back, Helen Kim eloquently addresses the audience. She then picks up her beloved on-loan million-dollar violin, surveys the crowd—eyes pausing on her proud and happy parents and younger siblings—smiles, breathes deeply, and begins to play. At first, I can't identify the song. But then Helen hits some very familiar notes, and I realize she's selected a classical arrangement of "Yankee Doodle"—a quintessentially American tune. I'm betting most of us in the room haven't heard it performed by a classical violinist, not to mention a virtuoso who recently won first place in a competition to discover the most gifted violinist under age eighteen in the United States.

A perfect choice, Helen, I think, as I look around the room and see smiling faces, many with tear-filled eyes. *A perfect choice for this joyous celebration.* And I also think, *We are so fortunate to have her here with us as a permanent resident.*

She finishes the song and bows as the audience applauds wildly. It's a moment I know I'll always remember and a culmination of hours of intense hard work and days and nights of deadline-induced anxiety. It's a festive gathering for Helen and her family, as well as for their friends and supporters, my law partner at the time Jeff Goldman, our legal team, and me. Today, we celebrate the arrival a few weeks earlier of green cards for Helen and her family, allowing them to stay in the country permanently, putting an end to a harrowing and deeply stressful immigration saga.

Helen says she too will never forget that party. "It was so exciting to go to the law firm, and I was honored that they asked me to perform," she says, years later as a young woman in her mid-twenties who earned a degree as a full-scholarship student at Harvard University and performs sold-out concerts all over the world. "It felt like a big family reunion. You know, sometimes when you go through really stressful times with people, even if you haven't known them for long, you feel like you know those people very well. That day was so joyous, and we felt so much relief; it was especially a huge relief for my parents."

As is customary for Helen, she demonstrated her distinctive humor during that period in her life. "When the green cards arrived, I emailed everyone involved in helping my family during that entire process," she recalls. "I wrote: 'Our yellow-green cards arrived!' I guess I didn't think they were green enough."

I must admit, like her parents, I released several sighs of relief after learning they received their green cards, and I was able to enjoy that celebratory concert at our law firm, proud of what we had helped Helen and her family accomplish. My colleagues also took pride in Helen and what we did to help her, with the full support of the firm. That evening, after the event, so many colleagues sent emails to Jeff and me commenting on how moved they were by the event, and the pro bono victory it represented. I still have one such email from one of our colleagues with the subject "Well done!" and the accompanying email text: "I am quite sure that I have never had a more positively moving experience at Mintz than this afternoon, seeing Helen, her family/friends and, of course, her stunning talents (violin being just one of them). I was so proud to work for Mintz. Thank you both." That comment serves as a good example of why I love my law firm.

But, mostly, I felt proud of all the work Helen had done as an incredibly mature preteen seemingly up to any task and serving as the official family liaison with our firm during the entire process, writing a pivotal letter to immigration officials, and helping her and her family's cause in so many other ways. What she did at her age was truly remarkable. Jeff and I had never seen anyone like her; she was and is an absolute genius!

An Enriching Childhood

Helen, her younger siblings, and her parents came to New York City when Helen was a young girl. Her mother was working on what's called an R-1 temporary work visa as a religious lay worker for an Asian church, which gave the rest of the family the ability to stay in the United States and attend school here, as her R-1 visa dependents. Helen's parents were excited that their children would benefit from the U.S. educational system, which they had long admired. Helen was born with the gift of perfect pitch, which is extremely rare. When she arrived in the United States, she was already a violin prodigy who had made her solo debut with an internationally acclaimed symphony orchestra at age six. Not surprisingly, Helen came to the attention of the Juilliard School of Music and was one of the youngest musicians ever admitted into the Juilliard Pre-College division. Had they stayed in their native Asian country, she never would have had this and so many other life-changing opportunities.

"I've come to realize just what an amazing education I got in the States," Helen now says. "Had I stayed in Asia, I think that the way I would have developed as a person, a musician, and a thinker would have been very different."

During her childhood in this country, Helen was deeply committed to studying violin and performing before audiences, participating in competitions, and winning many of them. She wouldn't have been able to achieve this success without the help of sponsors—those people who recognized her abilities and the organizations with which they were affiliated. For example, as a preteen, Helen became a recipient of From the Top's $10,000 Jack Kent Cooke Young Artist Award and appeared on both From the Top's NPR radio show and the PBS television series. She also received the Jack Kent Cooke Foundation's Young Scholars Award.

In receiving such attention as a prodigy violinist, Helen was obviously different from other kids; her unique intelligence and abilities combined with a diligent work ethic made her stand out, but she still had friends and did the things young preteens like to do.

"When I was a kid, it didn't occur to me that I was missing out on anything because I had so many experiences that others didn't have," she says. "I loved what I was doing. It was so enriching—and not just in an academic sense but in a very human way. Yes, it was stressful, and sometimes, I didn't have a lot in common with other students, but kids were always nice to me. I never felt like an outcast."

Her teachers loved her and treated her like she was older than her years, which enhanced her maturity level. "I was always popular with teachers and was friends with all of them. They gave me extra books to read. I'd help them clean up, and I'd get some of my emotional friendship happiness from them. I guess that's a nice way of saying that I was always the teacher's pet," she adds with a laugh.

Winning the Mad Dash

I first learned about Helen and her family on March 19, 2008, when they saw trouble on the horizon. Big trouble. Their New York–based immigration attorney had started work on their green card process based on Helen's mom's religious worker status, but that application was not far enough along to give them an independent basis to stay in the country and their lawful stay in R-1 and R-2 visas status was set to expire on March 26, making them all deportable. Even worse, he had stopped returning their increasingly frantic phone calls.

Having become close with the staff at From the Top, Helen told them about her family's dire situation and their need for immigration help. They also told them that they lacked the resources to hire a good law firm. Word quickly spread to the leadership and board members of From the Top. They reached out to me, as they knew that Mintz Levin has cultivated (and maintains) a strong commitment to pro bono work; consequently, they approached us at the eleventh hour when everything was breaking apart for the family. Getting that call pumped an adrenaline rush through me, because we were asked to save a family from possible—perhaps likely—deportation before it was too late.

I was so compelled to take the case that there was no way I could *not* take it. I just had to help this extraordinary girl and her family. They were on the verge of having the sky fall down on them. I guess it's something in my DNA and, frankly, also in the genetic composition of so many of my partners. If we think we might be able to do something for someone and we can find a team to help and gather the resources we need to get it done, we do it. My then-partner Jeff Goldman (who went on to success-fully launch and run his own immigration law firm) also takes a lot of pro bono cases, and he has a big heart, so I knew I'd have someone to embrace this cause with me and go all out to win. Theirs was such a sympathetic and compelling predicament that we were confident that many of our colleagues would also lend a helping hand if we needed them.

So, bodies and brain power weren't the problem; time was.

A case like this normally takes months to prepare. We had one week to marshal the resources, devise a strategy, tap our network of relationships, execute a plan, and file the case. Because it was such a sympathetic case and time was of the essence, the firm's Pro Bono Committee approved it with lightning speed. One hurdle cleared, many more to go.

Our legal team flew into action and worked frenetically around the clock—and that clock was ticking like a proverbial time bomb. After con-ducting conference calls with Helen, her family, and members of From the Top, I concluded that the best shot the family had to stay in the United States was to immediately petition for an O-1, extraordinary ability visa.

But that would only cover Helen. Could we save the rest of the family? Fortunately, Helen's father is an amateur musician and played a key role supporting her on-stage performances, which allowed us to request O-2 visa status for him and dependent authorized visa status for the rest of the family members. Thank goodness he was instrumental in her perfor-mances, because if he had not played an important role, we would have had no way to secure a visa for Helen's mother and siblings. It was only because her dad was intimately involved in her concerts that we were able to lay out a strategy that would take care of all five family members.

We also had to scramble during an intense few days to draft sup-port letters from some of the world's most renowned violinists, orchestra conductors, and music schools; gather evidence of Helen's many awards; and prove that she was the beneficiary of an astonishing loan from the Stradivari Society of that priceless violin—an instrument Helen would never let out of her sight; she even slept with it. Essentially, we needed to show that she was, indeed, extraordinary and would contribute to our culture. Over the course of five exhausting days, we received urgent FedEx packages with the signed supporting letters that we hoped would clinch our case.

In our one week of round-the-clock work—one of the more intense weeks of my career—we prepared and filed the application, which, if approved, would save this wonderful family and, if it was denied, would doom them. We all breathed a deep sigh of relief when the government notified us that it was approving, just in the nick of time, all of their applications. With the approval, the entire family transitioned from an imminently lapsing immigration status to another immigration status that would allow them to stay for several more years. If the visa approvals had taken one more day than they did, everything would have been different.

During a period lasting nearly two years, as we worked to gain permanent residency status for Helen and her family, we deployed a lot of creative thinking and, to borrow from football terminology, performed the requisite blocking and tackling. We worked closely with sympathetic contacts inside USCIS. And importantly, we had the support of the amazing Emily Winterson, who worked for years spearheading immigration cases in Senator Ted Kennedy's office and the offices of other prominent lawmakers, including Elizabeth Warren. Emily has a heart of gold. She's now retired, but she single-handedly helped thousands of deserving immigrants through her good work over many decades. In short, many people showed that they truly cared.

I mentioned the letter to immigration officials that Helen wrote in support of her parents to assert why she needed both of them with her here in the United States. It was very important, well written, sincere, and heartfelt. The two-page letter opens like this: "My mom and dad are my very best supporters. They love and care for me, and without them I would not be the artist I am today."

She goes on to demonstrate the ways in which her mother helps her and travels with her to the many concerts she performs, and then she shifts over to focus on her father; both parents get equal praise for the ways in which they're vital for her development as a musician, although we were more worried about her father being denied: "My daddy is very special. While my mom can be called my 'road' manager, my dad is my 'home' manager. He is also an amateur violinist, and he has ears that are trained for music. While my mom coaches me in the viewpoint of the audience, my dad has the viewpoint of a musician. He also technically helps me: He always thinks up new fingerings or bowing possibilities for me after he hears me practice."

She closes the letter with more gratitude and love: "I am proud to call these people my parents, my supporters, and my number one fans. I know that without the little things that they do to help me, I would not be here today in the United States."

Today, she talks about her role during that angst-riddled time and about writing the letter—showing the modesty that those who know Helen come to expect. "Our whole case for our family's green card rested on my role in the family. We had to make a strong case why neither of my parents' applications should be rejected. Once I knew what we were up against, I knew this time it was me who had to advocate for my parents and not the other way around. So I didn't really have a choice to be the liaison," she says and laughs. Then she adds, matter-of-factly, "There was no one else to write this letter. It needed to be done, so I just did it." I'm sure Helen's letter was crucial to our success in a case that was so complicated, with many moving parts and roller-coaster ups and downs.

Spreading Her Wings on the World Stage

Over the years since we won the case, my husband Michael and I developed an even deeper relationship with Helen and her family, and we have greatly enjoyed seeing her rise on the world stage. And the music that comes out of her heart and mind and through her hands and violin is nothing short of magical.

Michael and I have attended many of her performances. We flew down to Washington, DC, for her Kennedy Center debut and traveled to New York to see her first performance with the New York Philharmonic, at Lincoln Center in Avery Fisher Hall. There were people in her life who had been promoting Helen, supporting her along the way, and investing in her emotionally. Many of these folks also attend her performances, particularly the major concerts and debuts. After the performance in Avery Fisher Hall, many of us had dinner with her family, including some members of my family who I had invited to go to the concert. Everyone wanted to see this amazing girl that I'd been talking about so much. It's been very joyous to watch her spread her wings. We are all so proud of her.

I'm also proud of how she carries herself—with dignity, humility, beauty, and grace—and appreciates what this country has given her. She also recognizes just how arduous the path was that she and her family had to navigate, just as other immigrants have done and continue to do today, despite the increasingly difficult roadblocks—and often, cruelty—they encounter along their way.

"Most people don't know how hard it is to immigrate," she says. "Because the United States has historically been a hub of immigration, my story is not an unusual one. At the same time, it's difficult. I feel very grateful to have passionate, careful lawyers and other people who helped my family. I have a lot of friends who are amazing people, took all the right steps, and immigrated, but then had issues with their green cards and had to move back just because they didn't meet the right people or didn't have the resources."

She's absolutely correct. The vast majority of immigrants try to do everything the right way. They have the best intentions and they hire lawyers, but sometimes, the lawyers mess up (even with the best of intentions), or their case gets buried in the bowels of the bureaucracy, and their status becomes precarious—or worse.

Helen considers herself fortunate, because we were able to steer her case in the right direction, but she also realizes that others increasingly run into challenges in their immigration pursuits and often face raw discrimination and in-your-face hatred. "With the current political atmosphere, it's so much more difficult than ever," she says. "But for a lot of people, if there's a will, there seems to be a way. It's like a miracle. I think the people who try to immigrate to America tend to be persistent people. They want to venture out. And most immigrants have a sense of optimism: They crave a move to an unknown place, a big adventure."

Since she started studying violin at age four under the concertmaster of an internationally renowned orchestra, Helen's "big adventure" has taken her to countries and concert halls around the world, from Singapore to Italy to New York's Carnegie Hall and so many places in between. She studied in Germany and France and speaks German, French, and, of course, her native language, as well as English. Joke with her about *only* speaking four languages, and she'll laugh . . . and then quietly say, "Well, I can't speak Russian very well, but I love reading Russian poetry." She graduated from the Juilliard School and earned a degree in comparative literature at Harvard.

Committed to giving back to her community, she also volunteers her time. On several occasions, I've asked her and her brother, who's an excellent amateur cellist (her much younger sister plays piano), to perform a benefit concert for PAIR, and of course, they've always happily agreed to do it.

Feeling the Flow
While Helen loves meeting people and making new friends and she relishes her intellectual life—comfortable in virtually any social or academic environment—perhaps nowhere is she more at home, besides being with her family, than on stage in front of an appreciative audience.

So how does she feel when she's captivating and mesmerizing a concert hall full of people, when she's in the moment and in the spotlight? "I've never verbalized that before," she says after a long (for her) pause. "When you're in a concert, it almost feels like an out-of-body experience. My consciousness is, of course, inside my body, but there are two levels of consciousness, including a meta level that is perfectly aware of everything that is going on, and so I notice how my body is responding physically."

Another mental-emotional state manifests in a visceral and ephemeral way. "The other level feels more spontaneous. This is when I feel the freest on stage," she says, adding that she maintains control and the freedom to make changes as she so desires without overthinking her decisions. "Maybe it's what people call the 'flow.'"

And then there's yet another feeling she gets, fueled by a loose and wild neurotransmitter buzz. "There are certain musical pieces that fill us with a pure adrenaline response. In this case, there is no control. You just let it go, because you can't control it anyway. It's pure instinct. Those moments don't last very long. But for a minute or two, it's a pure rush. I suppose it's what Freud would call an 'oceanic feeling.'"

Off the stage, she often reflects on immigrants' contributions to the fabric of American life. "I think every person who lives in the States contributes to America," she says. "The more I travel, the more I truly believe that. This is a land of immigrants. Whether it's a person working at a dry cleaner or at a government post, we all work hard and contribute to this nation in different ways, which are all meaningful and necessary. Immigrants want to contribute because they're usually a product of other people who worked hard to help put them where they are. I know I am."

The first time I heard Helen perform was at her victory concert in our firm that April day in 2009. When she played "Souvenir d'Amérique" by Henri Vieuxtemps, which is essentially a virtuosic variation on "Yankee Doodle," it was very moving. It felt so gratifying and so right that the United States should be the new home for Helen and her family.

How lucky we are to have this person in our midst. She's truly a treasure.

UZBEKISTAN

TURKMENISTAN

AFGHANISTAN

IRAQ   IRAN

PAKISTAN

INDIA

CHAPTER 5

FEEDING THE HUNGER TO HELP:

AMID THREATS TO HIS LIFE, SOCIAL SCIENTIST GAINS POLITICAL ASYLUM AND CONTINUES TO HELP THOSE IN NEED

A t the end of the twenty-first century's first decade, fundamentalist, militant, antigovernment forces of a war-devastated, south-central Asian country delivered violent, intimating, and very clear messages to Nasir Osmani: They hated that he was educating girls and young women in a province they intended to dominate, instructing them in Western values, and—worst of all—teaching them to believe in their equality to men. Nasir represented a direct threat to their way of life, and he became their target.

In the province where Nasir was working (which was distant from his home near the capital), members of these antigovernment forces stopped Nasir's uncle and beat him badly with the back of a rifle. As his uncle lay writhing in pain on the ground, the terrorists delivered a dark message. They told him that they knew about Nasir. They knew he worked for a nongovernmental organization in partnership with the country's government, had studied in the United States, and had set up an organization to promote democratic political ideas and raise awareness among young people—something they believed undermined their fundamentalist objectives. They called Nasir an "agent of America." As soon as he recovered from this horrific beating, his uncle warned Nasir that his life was in danger and that he should limit his activities and stay close to his home near the capital, despite his strong desire to lift up the young people he so badly wanted to help.

While this violent attack certainly rattled Nasir, and he felt terrible that his uncle was harmed, at first, he essentially dismissed it as an isolated act that could only transpire in certain outer provinces controlled by antigovernment forces. "That time, I didn't take the warning as seriously as I later would, because the attack on my uncle happened outside of [the capital city], which has its own internal security," he told me a few years later, after he became my client. "I hoped that, if I stayed in my province, I'd be okay."

But the threats came closer. In fact, they came right to his house, hours away from the school where he was teaching. Soon after attacking his uncle, the terrorists started following Nasir around in an obvious, menacing way. The first time, a band of them entered the capital city (by itself unusual) and followed Nasir to the government ministry where he worked as a consultant. While that frightened him, his fears heightened two weeks later, when they tailed him a second time, clearly wanting to intimidate him even more. But then the threats hit home, literally. The rag-tag but well-organized and armed team of antigovernment mercenaries showed up at Nasir's family home, asking for him and his father, who had also been a progressive activist, although not to the extent that Nasir was.

He remembers this encounter vividly. "When they arrived at our home, the housekeeper went to see who was at the gate," Nasir says. "The housekeeper said the people who wanted to see us were very aggressive. We could see them from the second story of our house and noticed their distinctive cars and clothing, which told us they were antigovernment forces. It was a very nerve-racking situation. We told the housekeeper to tell them that my father and I were not at home and hoped this would be enough to get them to leave. This close call actually happened on two separate occasions. All of this was very alarming and made me realize that things were getting more and more serious."

Nasir's distress grew to a fevered pitch when a government official and family friend learned from informants that Nasir's name was on a list of those targeted to be killed by the terrorists. In addition, a devastating tragedy befell his community when a fellow youth activist, a student who had recently graduated, was kidnapped and murdered just two miles from Nasir's neighborhood.

Nasir wanted nothing more than to continue his important work in his country, but his life was in real danger, and he had no choice but to leave his country to stay alive. He was not the only one who was afraid: Ever since he learned that Nasir was on a kill list, his father was beside himself with worry for his son, each passing day fraught with ever-increasing anxiety.

Nasir knew he needed to devise and implement a plan to save his life. "I decided to go back to the United States and pursue my education in graduate school," he recalls, adding that he still managed the educational organization he founded. "In college, when I was earning my undergraduate degree, one of my professors knew people at the defense ministry and understood what was going on in the world. He told me it was better not to go back to my country. He said it was better for me to stay in the United States and continue my education. So, when all of these things started happening to me in my country, I remembered what he had told me."

Nasir applied to and was accepted into grad school at a top-tier American university in the Northeast. After he'd been there for some time, with mounting threats at home, he reached the point where he had to seek political asylum. "I talked with people in the international office [of the university] and told them that I needed protection," he recalls.

College advisors connected him with PAIR, and its volunteer attorneys screened Nasir, as they do all candidates for asylum, to make sure he met the requirements, such as being unable to afford a lawyer and having a bona fide asylum case. Satisfied that Nasir met those and other conditions, they then took the standard next step in the process and reached out to a volunteer lawyer in the Greater Boston community. That was me. I accepted the case, and I'm so glad I did.

Gaining a Passion for Social Change

I had read Nasir's profile and learned quite a bit about this incredible young man. He was born to a prominent family in his country, which was at war with a neighboring nation. His father, a scholar, published several books on the resistance to the bigger nation's occupation in the 1980s. When Nasir was a young child and the conflict between his native country and the occupying nation intensified, the family fled to the relative safety of another country. Although he spent much of his childhood as a refugee, he and his family relocated to their homeland after much of the danger had subsided, and he attended high school there.

"After decades of civil war, there was not much left of the infrastructure in my country," he says. "We had no windows in my high school. I studied on concrete in the winter. So many things were depleted in terms of resources, and I wasn't able to get the education I wanted. I then attended a college in the capital city and studied economics, but I wanted to get a better educational opportunity."

He started looking for colleges abroad that could satisfy his academic yearnings. "The United States scholarships were really the only ones available to those of us in a developing country," he says. "I applied, and I was lucky enough to be selected"—for a Fulbright scholarship, no less.

"I got the scholarship as an undergrad, and they usually only give them to postundergrads. But the U.S. embassy understood that there might be some undergrads who would have potential to grow and contribute. It was unbelievable, and I tried to make the best of it."

As a Fulbright scholar, Nasir came to the United States in the late spring of 2007 to continue his studies in economics at a progressive liberal arts college in the Midwest. Ask him what his first impressions were of the United States, and he doesn't hesitate to answer: American kindness—and cars.

He explains: "When I landed in California at the airport, I was very confused, and we had a delay, but a lady helped me with everything. She was just another passenger and didn't know me at all, but she was very helpful, especially after she found out this was the first time for me in the United States. When I got to the Midwest and rode on the highways to where my school was, I was really impressed with the variety of cars. I had never seen so many kinds of different cars in my life. I was trying to see if I could find two cars that were similar, but I couldn't. That was really the first thing that surprised me, and I remember thinking, *This is really different.*"

He was hit with another surprise—the academic standards and demands of the highly regarded college. "When school started, it was very different than what I expected," he says. "I thought it was going to be an easy journey, but it wasn't. I wasn't prepared for the academic rigor and all the requirements that I faced during my first year. It was tough. I always knew that the United States was the land of freedom and opportunity, but I discovered that you have to work really hard. I also learned firsthand why the United States is a world leader in so many areas. It's because of the work ethic of the people."

He discovered something else when talking to other foreign students studying in the U.S. "I also found that the people who select themselves to go to the United States want to achieve something, and they are also very hardworking."

During his studies, Nasir became passionate about social change in his homeland and hoped to apply his knowledge of economics to youth activism. "When I was in college, I thought a lot about what could change my country," he says. "A lot of people in the rural areas are uneducated and illiterate, especially the youth. Education is an enlightenment process. If the youth are not enlightened, they are more likely to be successfully recruited and brainwashed by antigovernment forces. So thinking along these lines—about education as a tool for change—was super powerful to me, and I would speak to my professors about it. We'd talk about when you look at developing countries, you see that those that had a huge jump in education also had a huge overall jump in development and in health and economic prosperity."

Narrowing His Demographic Focus

Well before his life became endangered, while on summer break from his academic program, Nasir returned to his country and worked for a nongovernmental organization (NGO) fighting global poverty. The nonprofit focused on the economic advancement of women and girls in the country, where entrenched political and societal structures often keep women from attending school and starting careers. This was something that he had already spent a lot of time thinking about, prompted in part by attending his Midwestern college classes alongside women, a first for him.

Consequently, he narrowed his focus on youth education to a demographic in dire need. "I would think about villages in my country where you have this whole gender that is not educated. I thought, *What if they were educated?*" he says. "I did a lot of research on this, and I came to understand that if you could educate the girls, it would have more impact than just educating the boys, because, later on, the woman becomes the central figure in the home."

While his philosophy is rooted in compassion, it's also centered on strategy—as he demonstrates by completing this thought as a true economist might: "So the return on the investment is much higher if you focus on educating women."

That summer, the NGO assigned Nasir to meet with community leaders, religious figures, and teachers in a northern province to discuss the highly controversial act of allowing girls in school. The results of Nasir's work were published by both the organization and the government.

In addition to his work at the organization, Nasir founded a youth educational organization to raise awareness and empower other youth leaders to advocate for social change. He was the founder and president of this organization and continued to advise the group after he returned to the U.S. to continue his academic program.

After he completed his degree, Nasir returned to his home country, and that's when he acted as a consultant to the governmental ministry in his work for the organization that helped support sustainable development, health, education, and good governance. And that's also when the threats against his family and his life began.

Fighting Bureaucratic Battles

During our first meeting regarding his political asylum case, I was struck immediately by how articulate and brilliant Nasir is. Second, I was equally impressed with his commitment to fostering education for girls and young women and trying to raise the consciousness for equality in education of the community he lived in. This constitutes a major component of his mission. I was truly awed by his commitment, his empathy, and his passion to educate disadvantaged girls and young women. Right away, he demonstrated to me that he's someone who is dedicated to making positive change in the world and very focused on using his life to better the lives of other people.

I knew I'd made the right decision to volunteer my time and take his case.

We were a good fit for what would become a long, hard fight. With the help of my team of Mintz Levin attorneys, we filed his asylum application and prepared Nasir for his asylum interview in front of a USCIS officer. After waiting the statutorily required period, we also applied for an employment authorization for Nasir, which we secured—but only after answering multiple requests for evidence by USCIS. And then the agency dragged its bureaucratic feet for months stretching into years, at times ghosting us.

We suspected that Nasir's country of origin was the reason for the government's silence and holdups. Often, for political asylum cases on behalf of people from certain countries, immigration officials don't treat them the same way as everyone else and don't seem to care how long it takes them. What's more, it doesn't matter what societal contributions the asylum candidate has already made or what concrete plans he or she has made to do more good for society. When asked, the government explains the extreme delays in processing applications for people from certain countries as being national security–based delays. But as far as I'm concerned, case processing delays that drag out to double and triple the time of everyone else's cases reek of profiling and outright discrimination. The proof of the pudding is in the eating. If there really was a national security–based reason not to approve someone's case, the government wouldn't issue the approval in response to being sued.

As these typical case-processing delays mount, anxieties rise. When this happens, people get stuck in limbo. They don't know what the outcome is going to be and can't plan their futures. They fear—and that's up-in-the-middle-of-the-night fear—they might get denied and forced to leave the United States. They wonder what will happen to them because they really would be in danger if they had to go home. They think about all their friends from other countries whose cases were approved so much more quickly. This was certainly the case for Nasir.

My team and I sent several requests for an update on Nasir's status, to no avail. Two years after his application was filed, we wrote and delivered another letter asking USCIS to adjudicate his case. USCIS responded that the case was still under officer review. Six months later, there was no USCIS action, and we sent a follow-up letter, which did not yield action. Finally, I reached a point where I had had enough.

I told Nasir, "Because it had gone far beyond the normal processing time to adjudicate your case, I'm drawing a line in the sand. I want to make sure that you agree and authorize it, but I want to file a lawsuit to compel them to make a decision on your application." He agreed, so that's what I did on December 15, 2014. In response, the asylum office approved his case a couple days later, on December 18, nearly three years after we filed the case, proving that, sometimes, to get results on legal issues, you have fight forcefully with litigation fire.

I called Nasir, told him we had some good news, and asked if he'd come to my office. Telling him that we'd won the case was a magical moment—for all of us. Here's how Nasir remembers it: "I found out from Susan in her office, and it happened right before Christmas. I thought, *Well, this is the perfect gift for the end of the year*. I felt reborn, like I had been given a second chance to live. I felt welcome in America and integrated into society. And then Susan and I celebrated with her colleagues at a happy and festive dinner."

I like to think of experiences like these as points of light.

I feel lucky to have my friendship with this brilliant, compassionate man. I have introduced him to my family, and he's come over for Thanksgiving. My husband, Michael, and I attended his master's degree graduation, and PAIR even invited him to serve on its board, which he did for a number of years. No matter what the future brings, we will always be family.

Using Social Science to Help the Poor

As the beneficiary of an approved asylum application, Nasir was able to apply for permanent residency within one year. Soon after, he became a permanent U.S. resident.

The violence in his home country continues, and in 2016, Nasir received horrible news. A man who had helped Nasir's youth education organization and other groups that worked toward improving people's lives was assassinated outside of his home with a bomb. The authorities determined that he was killed by antigovernment forces. "When I found out about this, it was a huge shock; he was very active in helping people—and he was a mentor to me," Nasir says. "I realized that, if this person could be assassinated so easily, then any person who is active could also be a target for assassination."

Nasir earned his master's degree from the New England grad school, and he's working as a social scientist and researcher for a major Midwest university. Right before this book went to print, Nasir successfully defended his dissertation and proudly graduated with his doctorate. You can hear the passion and determination in his voice when he talks about his goals. "It's all about focusing on the people in society who have the least resources," he says. "You can uncover a lot of reality through social science research. One goal of mine is to see how I can help both developing countries as well as poor people in the United States."

He has crafted his own research specialty: the ramifications of shock—through natural disaster, war, tragedy, and anything that upends people's lives—and how it affects families. "I study what the behavior is, the thinking processes, and decision-making," he says. "Once we know the behaviors, we can come up with better policies to help them through the shock. And poor people feel the most brunt of a shocking experience. They are the most vulnerable, and they suffer the most. So I'm studying households that have few resources. This is research that can be applied in the United States and all over the world. I want to do what I can to help."

CHAPTER 6

WAITING FOR THE HAMMER TO HIT HOME:

A LONG SUCCESSFUL JOURNEY AMID
INEPTITUDE, FEAR, AND ANXIETY

Virtually all immigrants experience low points, times that drag them down deep into despair. Often, this feeling manifests in a very bad day, one they want to bury in the backyard. Jacque Colon has lived through several of these awful days since she came to the United States from the Dominican Republic, embarking in 1997 on a twenty-year struggle to gain U.S. permanent residency. Hers was a journey packed with indescribable anxiety.

That's right: The immigration process for this strong, successful, and determined woman took two difficult decades.

While Jacque maintains an upbeat approach to life, guided by her deep love of her two daughters and unwavering religious faith, she points to several dark times along the way to securing residency. She recalls the many times the lawyers she engaged performed truly shoddy legal work or failed to do anything at all, placing her immigration status in jeopardy and setting her back financially. One in particular failed her repeatedly. "I was paying a lot of money, and he didn't do anything with my case,"

Jacque says. "He didn't even check—nothing. For years, all he did was ask me for more money and more money."

She remembers when her oldest daughter Ana was accepted to a prestigious private high school in a U.S. Northeast city but had to decline to attend because Jacque didn't feel safe submitting the necessary paperwork. Exhibiting the type of fear and caution that many immigrants feel, as well as deep parental anguish, she worried that something might go wrong if she provided detailed information about her and her family. "Even though I was paying my taxes and never got anything from the government, not even food stamps," she says, and pauses, "I didn't want to take any chances and do anything that could get me separated from my daughters."

Both Ana and Jacque's youngest daughter, Paola, had received permanent resident status through their biological father, who was a U.S. citizen. Jacque wanted them to have a life in the United States, with all of the opportunities this nation offers, and not be forced to go with her if she were ever deported, which was a very real possibility.

Among those dire days, however, one stands out as the worst, the day that Jacque hit rock bottom.

Bureaucratic Blunders

First, it's important to understand how Jacque's immigration application should have gone and all the things that she did right and the government did wrong. Jacque was eligible for a green card because of her marriage to her second husband, who, like her first husband, was a U.S. citizen. When someone gets a green card based on marriage to an American citizen, where the couple has been married for less than two years at the time the green card is granted, the green card is conditional; it's valid for only two years. Before the two years are up, the conditional green card holder must apply to USCIS to remove the conditions on the card and make it permanent once and for all. In the second application, the applicant has to show that he or she is still married and submit proof that the married couple is continuing to commingle their assets, live together, file joint tax returns, etc.

Jacque and her husband duly filed the application to remove the conditions on her green card, but after they filed it, they moved to a new home. One of the most important things that an immigrant must do is notify the government if she has changed residences, by submitting a change of address update to the immigration service within ten days of moving. This way, the government always knows where to find them (assuming the government properly processes the address update, a task at which the government fails more often than it cares to admit).

While waiting for the immigration authorities to make a decision on her permanent green card request, Jacque properly notified the government in writing of her address change. Indeed, throughout the entirety of her time in the United States, Jacque had taken all the good-faith steps to stay in this country legally as she worked to gain and retain permanent resident status. In fact, because she was so concerned that she never heard back from the Immigration and Naturalization Service (INS, the government agency that was the precursor to USCIS), she made numerous inquiries and proactively notified the agency on five different occasions of her change of address.

Despite all these efforts to communicate with the agency, she never got an answer on her application. She ended up waiting for years and years, and, eventually, her marriage broke down, and she and her husband divorced. Now, she was no longer married to an American citizen.

As it turned out, the agency had wanted to interview Jacque and her husband a second time before deciding her permanent green card application. Despite all the proper steps that Jacque took to inform the government about her new address, they sent a notice to her former address, instructing the couple to appear for an interview. It was not until years later that we found out that this government notice was returned back to the government and never forwarded to Jacque, so she had no idea that a second interview had ever been scheduled. Even though it was the government that was at fault, the consequences of missing that interview were catastrophic.

Her attorney at the time was unhelpful, but he did find out one piece of information that, for Jacque, was one of the most devastating shocks of her life. He told her that unbeknownst to her, years earlier, the INS had issued Jacque a notice to appear in immigration court for a deportation hearing. She couldn't believe her ears. Despite filing the proper paperwork, despite her myriad good-faith written inquiries and numerous updates that she provided to the government, and despite retaining a lawyer to help her get to the bottom of her pending application, it wasn't until many years had gone by that she found out that she'd been scheduled for—*and missed*—a deportation hearing.

Of course, you can't appear at a hearing if you don't know about it. When Jacque didn't show up for the hearing, the government hit her with an outstanding *in absentia* order of removal from immigration court, creating an incredibly scary and stressful situation for her. Paralyzed with fear that she'd be deported and separated from her beloved daughters, she enlisted the help of yet another immigration attorney to file a motion to reopen and reconsider her case. The government denied this motion in late 2007.

Soon after that, a piece of mail sent Jacque plummeting to her deepest emotional low. "One terrible day, I got a letter from the lawyer saying he couldn't do anything, that I just needed to wait for the immigration officials to show up, detain me, and send me back to the Dominican Republic," she recalls. "I didn't know what to do. I cried and cried and prayed and prayed."

And she waited—for years, as it turned out, with the surreal specter of detention and deportation looming on the horizon. This state of limbo constantly put Jacque's optimistic attitude to the test.

College or Bust

Both before and after Jacque received that ominous letter, she worked. And worked. Diligently. At a wide array of jobs, deeply motivated by an important goal. "I told myself that if I have to work twenty-four hours a day, I will do it so that Ana and Paola can go to college, because I know both of them wanted to become someone important and get careers that would let them help other people," she says. "I said to them, 'No matter what I have to do, I want you to go to college.' They wanted to go to college too, and they were very good students."

To provide a strong and stable environment for her daughters, Jacque toiled in a factory building computers, served as a caregiver to an elderly woman, cleaned houses, worked in a laundromat, sold Avon products, and held positions as a receptionist, administrator, and office manager, among other jobs. And she steeled herself emotionally both before and after the motion was denied, trying as best she could to hide the omnipresent anxiety she felt.

"I had to keep myself strong for my family," she says, "and I didn't want to give my daughters the stress I felt, which got worse after I received that letter and waited for them to take me away, put me on a plane, and send me back to the Dominican Republic. There were so many things in my head, and it was awful, with many years of living on the edge every single day. I didn't know where to turn or where to go."

Eventually, the waiting came to an end when, one day, three Immigration and Customs Enforcement agents came to Jacque's front door. Yet, unlike the horror stories you often hear about ICE, especially during the Trump administration, the female agent and two male agents extended compassion to Jacque.

"It might sound crazy and weird, but that was the beginning of [a series of] high points for me," Jacque says, explaining that, as she looked out the window and saw the agents' car pull up in front of her house, she knew they were coming for her, but she also knew that the years of waiting for this dreaded moment were over. And, somehow, she remained hopeful: "Deep inside of me, I was so in peace, and I knew that something good was going to come out of it. How? I didn't know. Who would help me? I didn't know—at the time."

The ICE agents informed Jacque that an order for her deportation had been issued because she'd missed that courtroom hearing several years ago. The female agent wanted to hear Jacque's reason for why she missed the appointment and asked to hear her story. Jacque poured her soul out to these immigration agents. She would soon realize, however, that the government already knew all about her. They'd done their homework, and they'd learned of Jacque's work ethic, her community service, and her devotion to her daughters' well-being.

"The lady agent knew everything about me," Jacque says. "She knew where I worked; she knew the church that I went to; she knew the time I was coming in and going out of my house. Everything. So there was nothing new that I was telling them. But one thing that she told me was 'Don't take this as something that isn't going to be good, because, finally, things will start moving for you. Instead of just sitting there with nothing happening, things are going to start going in the right direction.' And that's exactly what happened."

Ana was in college in Ohio when her godmother called to tell her that ICE had arrived at her family's house to question her mother and serve her papers. "My heart dropped when I heard that," Ana says, adding that she feared the worst and considers that to be the lowest point she ever experienced during her mother's immigration struggle.

Much later, when she heard the reaction of the ICE agents, she deduced that they considered her mother to be an ideal citizen—or unofficial citizen, that is. "I can imagine ICE agents looking into this woman's story," Ana says, "and saying to themselves and each other, 'Wait a minute. This woman tried to do everything right. She's hardworking; does service in her church; volunteers to help those who need food, clothing, and furniture; fills her house with people—often those in need—and takes care of them.'

"My mother is very well known in her community. The ICE agents probably thought that there's no reason to deport somebody like this. They already knew I was in Ohio at college and on a full scholarship. They knew my sister was a straight-A student. It was crazy how much they knew about us."

The potential deportation would not happen immediately, and, in the meantime, the government required Jacque to check in every month at an ICE check-in center nearby, under supervision, where, often, she'd be greeted by the female agent who came to her house to tell her about the deportation orders. Each time, before the agent dealt with Jacque, she'd remove any firearms from holsters and hand them to another officer. "That officer asked her why she was doing that, and the female agent said, 'Because I'm not going to use a weapon on her,'" Jacque recalls. "I was always treated with respect by her."

In September 2014, Ana, who had been living in the United States under a permanent resident status, became a U.S. citizen. She immediately filed a green card petition for her mother, which was approved by USCIS in early 2015 and would open the door for Jacque to become a permanent resident. Well, it would open it a crack, because one major impediment blocked her path through that doorway to what would be a liberating status and a life without worry in the United States. She needed to get the removal order reopened and rescinded—not an easy task.

Hours of Research Pay Off

Soon after that, in 2016, Jacque and Ana reached out to me and my team at Mintz Levin. It was a bit daunting to realize that we represented her last hope to clear this final hurdle. Ana was working in Senator Elizabeth Warren's office, where she met Emily Winterson, an immigration specialist for more than three decades in the Boston Senate offices of Senators Edward Kennedy, Paul Kirk, and Scott Brown, as well as Warren. Emily gave my name to Jacque and Ana.

At our first meeting, Jacque described the whole ordeal as a "nightmare" and wanted to ensure that she could remain in the United States with her daughters. I was touched by Jacque's horrific saga, and, frankly, I was also angered by the government's mishandling of the immigration process and her attorneys' bungling of the legal matters. I instantly liked Jacque—her intelligence, warm personality, strong work ethic, and, of course, her steadfast love for her daughters—and, naturally, I agreed to take the case.

My team and I sprang into action. First, we tried to determine if the *in absentia* order that Jacque received was in fact lawful and valid. I suspected it may have been improper, because, by law, such an order is only authorized and proper if the respondent *receives* the warnings and advisements contained in a notice to appear. I had to find some evidence that Jacque did not, in fact, receive them, so I spent hours and hours reviewing the court files and government records in her case.

Finally, I found evidence of the government's failure—the smoking gun. The government files contained several official envelopes from the immigration court containing Jacque's notice to appear for her deportation hearing and other correspondence from the immigration court addressed to Jacque, all clearly stamped *Not deliverable* and returned to the government. Despite all of Jacque's many years of good-faith and proper efforts to update the government about her change of address, the U.S. government never properly updated its own records, repeatedly and recklessly failing her, and then tried to remove her because of the government's own internal administrative errors. We had the proof in hand.

In February 2017, our team filed another motion to reopen and rescind the removal order and put together a boatload of very detailed supporting documents, which demonstrated, among other things, uncontestable evidence that Jacque had taken proper steps on five separate occasions between February 2001 and March 2003 to update USCIS about her change of address and to ask the government about the status of her case.

When my team went to court to make our case, the judge took one look at the filing and said he was inclined to grant the motion to terminate removal proceedings immediately. Tellingly, the government attorney didn't raise a fuss and made no effort to oppose the motion. This, by itself, is quite rare. In the end, it was an open-and-shut case. So in a few short minutes, at the one hearing Jacque appeared at because she actually knew it was happening, her years of fear and anxiety were coming to close.

As a result of our team's efforts, finally, Jacque's deportation case was reopened, her removal order was rescinded, and, based on Ana's green card petition on her mother's behalf, Jacque received the immigration status she'd been seeking all these years. She attained the holy grail: She became a lawful permanent resident on May 18, 2017.

Fêting Freedom from Fear, Pursuing Dreams

We needed to party! So, soon after we won the case, Jacque, Ana, Emily Winterson, some of my legal teammates, and I joined together for a tearful and ecstatic celebration at a fantastic Italian restaurant. Jacque was very happy and relieved, and, although she emanated so much emotion and joy she could hardly talk, she thanked us all profusely. I recall thinking how wonderful it was that, after a long, twenty-year immigration process, she could finally live her life without fear of deportation. I also couldn't help but think that, because she did everything right all along the way, she never should have been subjected to this kind of distress in the first place. What's more, the proof that would ultimately vindicate her had been sitting collecting dust in her file for years.

Ana says she often reflects on that joyous dinner. "When we were eating that great Italian meal, they were all talking, and I wasn't saying much of anything—except for thanking them, of course," Ana says. "I was also thinking, *These people have absolutely no idea how they have changed the trajectory of my life completely.* Because when you're a child of an immigrant whose status is not secure and you're a child who feels like, in some ways, you're the head of the household, you have to think about everybody and their well-being. So to simply know that my mom was going to be okay and able to stay with us made me feel much less burdened. It made me feel that things were going to be fine and that I could actually continue to pursue my dreams. I didn't know how to express that feeling, but I felt at peace and very grateful."

Both of Jacque's daughters are seeking to fulfill their ambitions. Paola earned a degree in health studies and is studying to become a nurse. Ana says her sister's goal is rooted in Paola's early years of separation when she stayed with other family members in the Dominican Republic until she could joyfully reunite with her mother and sister in the United States. "Paola is introverted, but she's extremely gentle and nurturing," Ana says. "She wants to be able to help people under a lot of stress feel extremely safe, nurtured, and cared for. And she is so good at those things. During any time of crisis, I know I can call my sister, and she'll make me chill out and feel taken care of."

As for Ana, after earning a degree in political science, Spanish, and dance, she worked on a number of political campaigns, including those of Barack Obama, Elizabeth Warren, and Senator Ed Markey. She also served as Warren's press assistant and later as a deputy political director, doing her part to help the Massachusetts senator win reelection in 2018.

Then Ana joined the labor movement as deputy communications director for Service Employees International Union (SEIU) Local 509 and later became the political coordinator for SEIU's Local 32BJ, where she taught civic engagement and social justice classes to the membership and executed public relations plans, among other things.

In 2020, Ana ran for mayor of Lawrence, Massachusetts, and while she dropped out of that race to support another candidate, I'm sure she'll continue to be involved in local politics and to contribute in important ways to our democratic system of government. She believes that "the backbone of democratic politics is civic engagement, education, and access," as she puts it.

As for Jacque, she beams when talking about her daughters. "I'm so proud of their accomplishments," she says. "I can see how they have become women who are doing well for themselves, but they are also helping others. So yes, I am very thankful and very proud of the two of them."

Both Ana and Paola recognize the love and support that Jacque has given them and will continue to give them, and they are very grateful for her. "My success," Ana says, "—and my younger sister's success—is a direct reflection of my mother's sacrifices and her vision of what it means to accomplish the American dream."

CHAPTER 7

OVER MOUNTAINS, ACROSS AN OCEAN, AND IN THE COURTS:

PEASANT FARMER SMUGGLED OUT OF CHINA WINS IMMIGRATION CASE

I couldn't bear the suspense any longer.

After waiting hours to hear about my client, I picked up the phone and called the Immigration and Naturalization Service detention center. I asked for Peng Xu, providing his date of birth and the number the INS had assigned him, as they do all detainees. "What is Peng's status, please?" I asked on that hot and humid afternoon in August 1993.

"Oh yes, the Chinese fellow," an INS officer said. "We released him two hours ago."

"You did WHAT?!"

"We let him go. He's a free man . . . for now."

"But he doesn't speak English; he can't read any street signs; he has no way to call me or his uncle in New York; he's never been to Boston before; he's never been in the United States before!" I tried to restrain my anger. "I specifically asked you to let me know if you were going to release him—*BEFORE* you released him—so that I could come and get him. And you said you would."

"That's not my problem, ma'am," the officer said. "Look, you should just be happy that we let him go."

I hung up the phone and worried. I worried about Peng, a Chinese peasant farmer seeking political asylum, wandering around lost and alone in this large, fast-paced city with no way to reach me and no way for me to reach him. I worried I'd never find him, never see him again. I especially worried about his safety. I had to act and act quickly.

Authorities Come Down Hard

Growing up poor in a rural province in southern China, Peng dropped out of school at the age of fourteen to help his family and work the fields. Eventually, he met a young woman, and they fell in love, married, and had a daughter—not considered optimal in his culture because girls are generally not as strong in the fields—and then they had another child, a son who was born deaf. By that time, even though China had already instituted its draconian one-child policy, the local authorities had not educated the villagers about birth control, and the rules were not at all clear. Indeed, in some remote farming villages, a second child was sometimes allowed, but the local official required a couple to wait ten years before attempting to have a second child. After their son was born, however, Peng and his wife suffered the consequences.

When the authorities learned that Peng and his wife had disregarded the one-child rule—perhaps because they didn't fully understand it—they hit the couple with an exorbitant fine, which amounted to more money than Peng could earn in a year, a sum he couldn't possibly pay. He gave them their life savings, which amounted to only half of the fine amount. This was not good enough, and the officials went into their home. They took away all their furniture and threatened to put Peng in jail until his neighbors banded together and convinced the local officials that the only way he'd ever be able to pay the rest of the fine would be if he could get a job that paid better than farming. Amazingly, the officials saw the logic in this.

Even though it was a terrible situation, Peng was able to secure a construction job through the help of a relative outside the village. He left his young family and moved away to try to earn enough to pay off the fine and hopefully get his furniture back. His wife and young children had no choice but to move back in with her parents. After one year of nonstop work away from his family, Peng was able to earn enough money to pay the balance of the fine, and he and his young family were reunited. It had been a difficult period, but it could have been much worse. Unfortunately, he and his family were soon going to find out how much worse the government's punishments could be.

After Peng was fined, the local officials required his wife (and all the other women in the village) to use birth control. Life resumed to normal, but his wife's health was not the same after the fining incident and their long separation. She was often unwell. Then in 1992, agitated and upset, she confided to him that the birth control device must have failed, because she was pregnant again. They knew that it was absolutely forbidden to have a third child. No one else in their village had ever had more than two children. But they were so worried about her health and felt certain that an abortion would be very dangerous for her. So, despite the government's policy, they decided to have the baby.

Soon after they made this decision, Peng learned that a man in a neighboring village, whose wife had a third child, was arrested and sentenced to jail and hard labor for five years. They became very frightened. Somehow, word of Peng's wife's third pregnancy got out, and he and his wife received a written notice delivered to their home, requiring her to report to the local clinic for an abortion. They knew if she didn't show up when required, the local officials would come to their home and forcibly take her to the clinic against her will. They were very frightened and had no choice but to act quickly. The very next day, Peng's wife fled with their two children to her mother's home in a neighboring village. They decided he would not go with them; it was better to try to divide their risks. So he stayed put.

It didn't take long before a large group of angry officials stormed into Peng's house to take his wife for the forced abortion. When they discovered she'd fled, they became even more irate and started to beat Peng and pull him outside, and they took sledgehammers and started wildly bashing in the house—intent on completely destroying it. The same kindly neighbors who had helped Peng before interceded yet again, trying to stop the officials, and in the ensuing melee and confusion, one of the neighbors spirited him away to his house. He hid there in a panic for a few hours, but he was so worried about putting his helpful neighbor at risk that he ran away and slept in a field that night.

The next day, Peng took a train and a bus to a far away village where his uncle lived. He got to his uncle's in a state of shock. While he stayed with his uncle, Peng's wife sometimes called the phone in the local village barbershop, where his uncle worked (most people in rural China didn't have phones at that time), to tell him to warn Peng that it was not safe for him to come back. Although he desperately missed his wife and children, the horrible reality sank in that he could never safely go back to see his family again. And he wouldn't be there for the birth of his third child. After a few months had passed, his wife passed instructions to Peng's uncle that the family had arranged for Peng to be smuggled out of China to the United States. Another uncle in upstate New York would take him in.

Snakehead Smugglers

So in the spring of 1993, he met up with the smugglers, known as *snakeheads,* who fabricate or alter passports and employ other means to transport people out of the country, often to Taiwan, Japan, Australia, Europe, Canada, and the United States, the destination Peng chose.

Peng joined a small group of others whose lives were also threatened, and, together, they embarked on a long journey on foot over treacherous mountains and into Burma (now known as Myanmar). They hiked for two days and nights with not much more than what they were wearing, a change of clothes, a few other possessions, and fake but authentic-looking passports safely tucked away in small cloth bags. Peng also had a ragged piece of paper with his New York–based uncle's name and phone number written in Chinese characters. "I remember that we were all climbing the mountains, and we had nothing to eat," he says. "During that time, I really thought I wouldn't make it. But with family on our minds, we powered through and climbed over to a place where someone picked us up."

Once in Burma, Peng had to wait three more months for the rest of the smuggling fee to be paid by the family before a new smuggler accompanied him on a series of flights, ending in a flight to the United States. After taking five different flights, he landed at Boston's Logan Airport on, of all days, July 4. During his four-month odyssey, he often thought he'd die en route, and, in the States, he feared he'd be deported to China, where the government would likely jail him and subject him to years of hard labor, or worse. "I was very scared each time I got on an airplane, because I didn't know English, and I was really afraid of being sent back to China by the American police," he says.

Once in the Logan Airport terminal, Peng followed the instructions the snakehead had given him: Find a men's room, tear up the passport, flush it down the toilet, and hide in a bathroom stall for three hours. Soon after he emerged from his hideout, he encountered an INS officer and begged him, as best he could, to let him stay because he was fleeing for his life and wanted political asylum. But his plea efforts were to no avail, and with one long and arduous physical voyage behind him, he was now embarking on what would become a protracted and difficult legal journey.

The INS took him into custody and placed him behind bars, where he was expected to stay until an asylum hearing could be scheduled for him in Boston Immigration Court. INS gave Peng access to an interpreter and a list of organizations he could call to try to get legal help. Fortunately for Peng, PAIR was included on that list.

Meeting Peng, Promising Full Support

Our firm has a unique and highly competitive project analyst program for gifted college grads. Every year, we hire a class of these project analysts to work at our firm for a two-year period and to rotate through different legal departments and gain in-depth exposure to our work. These motivated, brilliant, and hardworking colleagues often prove to be absolutely invaluable. In early August, one of the firm's project analysts, Laurie Hauber, was serving with us following her graduation from Harvard, where she concentrated in East Asian studies. Laurie spoke Mandarin, and she received word of Peng's case from PAIR.

"The case came to me, and I knew immediately that I wanted to work on it, because, for one reason, I've always been interested in international studies," Laurie recalls, adding that she thought her Mandarin skills, albeit only a little better than average at best, would be beneficial.

"I went straight to Susan, because she was obviously the attorney to work on something like this, and, of course, she was enthusiastically interested." She pauses and continues. "I had no idea at the time how influential this would be to my career path. It was, in large part, that case that inspired my decision to attend law school and become a lawyer." Laurie has since gone on to have a successful career in the legal and academic professions.

When I heard that, I wasn't surprised. Mintz fosters a nonhierarchical, bottom-up approach. Regardless of whether someone is a lawyer, legal assistant, or project analyst, if there is a pro bono legal project they are passionate about, the firm encourages them to bring the project to the firm's attention. And, on many occasions over the decades, nonlawyers have generated major pro bono opportunities and meaningful experiences for the entire Mintz community. And in that spirit, when Laurie told me about Peng and his case, I embraced his cause and wanted to do everything in my power to secure asylum for him and, I hoped, to one day reunite him with the family he had never wanted to leave behind.

I first met with Peng at the INS detention center. It was a challenge communicating with him, because he came from a province in rural China where everyone speaks a rare Chinese dialect. He didn't speak very much Mandarin, and it took the INS considerable effort to find an interpreter who could speak his dialect. They couldn't find anyone qualified in Boston and had to bring an interpreter up from New York City.

With the help of the interpreter, I immediately conveyed to Peng that I would help and fight for him without charging him anything. He was visibly moved, quite surprised to hear this, and thanked me profusely. The next thing I told him was that we'd have to go to court and convince an immigration judge to grant him asylum, which would require a lot of energy and effort. I let him know we'd be spending a lot of time together so that my legal team and I could understand everything that had happened to him and his family. My first goal, I told him, was to do all I could to get him released from detention.

Before I left him that first day, I also told Peng that I knew he had been worrying and under tremendous stress for months if not years. I encouraged him to trust that, going forward, I'd make securing his future my top priority, and I told him I hoped he might be able to relax a little bit, knowing that someone else would be looking out for his legal case. That seemed to comfort him.

I knew what else would provide solace—familiar nourishment. I had learned that the INS guards were not feeding Peng food he was used to— namely and most importantly, simple white rice. Just before I left, I asked politely but firmly that they serve him rice, vegetables, and some sort of protein for at least one of his three meals a day. Later, Laurie confirmed that they complied with my request. "That gave him some comfort while he was held in this very scary confinement center, not knowing what would happen to him," Laurie recalls.

Seeking Release from Detention

When I got back to the office that day, I focused all of my attention on Peng's case. His first hearing date in the immigration court was set for November 23, 1993. That was in three months, and there was no way I was going to let him sit behind bars in the detention center. I felt strongly that Peng was eligible for release, because he had articulated a credible case for asylum, meeting the criteria for release for those who can demonstrate a reasonable fear of persecution in their home country. I represented him at his reasonable fear interview, which would determine whether he'd be released from custody pending his asylum hearing. Peng's reason for fleeing China was so clear-cut to me. It seemed indisputable that he had already been persecuted and also that he had a well-founded fear of further persecution for failure to adhere to the Chinese government's one-child policy (in other words, "on the basis of political opinion," one of the five acceptable grounds for asylum).

But the INS disagreed. The district director of the Boston INS office wrote me a letter, which I opened with high hopes for good news. Instead, I was bitterly disappointed and quite sad. The director wrote that he had personally reviewed Peng's file and found that he didn't qualify for release on parole. In my view, the INS was dead wrong in this interpretation, especially because U.S. immigration policy regarding China's one-child rule had recently evolved. It called for a legal presumption to be exercised in favor of someone who had been harmed by China's one-child policy.

And clearly, Peng had been severely harmed, and his family was continuing to suffer under the Chinese government and its brutal enforcement of that draconian policy.

I wrote to the INS putting them on notice that I believed their interpretation was incorrect and that Peng deserved to be released until his hearing, based on the current state of U.S. policy on this issue. I stated firmly that if they did not release him, I would take the issue to a higher level.

The day after I sent my letter, I called the detention center and told them that I was appealing the decision to keep Peng behind bars. I was told that they had taken my letter under advisement and would decide that day whether or not to release him, and they promised to let me know the outcome. I reminded them that he spoke no English, and that's when I begged them to call me first if the decision was made to release Peng, so I could come and pick him up myself. They agreed in no uncertain terms that they would.

Scouring the City

After my phone conversation with the dismissive INS officer, who casually told me that they had released Peng "several hours ago," I was absolutely livid. I couldn't believe the recklessness of the INS officers in turning him out into the streets of Boston, despite previously assuring me that they'd contact me before releasing him. How could he possibly navigate Boston? What would become of him?

I took a deep breath and got to work quickly. We had no time to lose. I called an emergency meeting of my law clerks and project analysts, including Laurie, who had been diligently helping me on all aspects of Peng's case, including our budding legal defense strategy. With her shining intelligence, piercing analysis, enthusiasm, patience, and ability to communicate in Mandarin, Laurie became a critical member of his defense team.

I gathered the team together in my office and told them what happened. Laurie was particularly shocked and upset. "I remembering telling Susan, 'Oh my gosh, they released him without you there? Oh no!'" Laurie recalls. "I fell into a panic."

Even though I was still an associate at my law firm, during our meeting, I asked the two law clerks and Laurie to ask the partners whose cases they were working on for permission to take the rest of the day off from their other projects because we had a major emergency on our hands. I needed all hands on deck. We had to find Peng. I gave them each a copy of his photo so they could focus on his physical appearance and identify him. We quickly formed a plan for each of us to fan out across the city to all the bus depots and the train station to see if anyone could find him. Because only Laurie spoke Mandarin—which Peng hardly understood, but even a little would help—we agreed that we would show him a picture of me and use hand gestures to try to convince him to accompany whoever found him back to the office.

Then the four of us set out on our mission, hearts beating fast.

We scoured the neighborhoods around the INS office and beyond in pursuit of Peng. I raced around in a panic, my adrenaline propelling me forward. Amazingly, within an hour of leaving my office, I found him standing aimlessly in the Peter Pan Bus Station with a ticket in his hand; to this day, I don't know how he managed to find the station and purchase a ticket to upstate New York, where his uncle lived.

I was carrying a copy of his release documents with me, and between that and my urgent pointing, waving, gesturing, and gesticulating—I must have been quite a sight for passersby—he figured out I wanted him to come with me. He stared down at his ticket and outside at the bus, reluctant, as he truly wanted to see his uncle, and the bus was supposed to be leaving shortly. But I needed him to come back to my office so we could plan out the next steps of his case. I ended up pulling on his sleeve as if to say, "You have to come with me." I basically cajoled him out of the bus station, and then I called my helpers and asked that we reconvene.

"We were amazed and relieved that Susan found him, and we rushed back to the office from locations across the city," says Laurie, who was not far from the bus station, so she met Peng and me there, and the three of us walked back to my office together. "As we traversed the streets of Boston toward Susan's office, I felt that, in a sense, we were seeing the world through his eyes, which was more than mind-blowing. It was impossible to process. What we take for granted! He'd never seen a tall building before. He was so disoriented, and yet he was also wonderfully in awe."

First-Ever Experiences

And then we came to the entrance to the marble lobby of the skyscraper housing the Mintz offices, and Peng encountered something else he'd never seen before. "I didn't even think about this, but of course he didn't know what a revolving door is," Laurie says. "I motioned for him to go first, and he just stood there and didn't know what to do. So I went in first, and he crowded in right behind me in the same little compartment. He'd never been exposed to a contraption like this before. I should have had more emotional intelligence and explained it to him as best I could. It was so absurd, and I had to suppress laughter."

Once we were back in my office, Laurie tried to communicate with him, but it was difficult. We decided we needed help: A translator who spoke either English or Mandarin and Peng's dialect was not an easy person to find. We had at least an outside shot at finding someone to translate because my office is located next to Boston's Chinatown neighborhood.

So we decided to walk the streets of Chinatown with Peng to search for someone who spoke his dialect.

It was well into the evening by now, and with a somewhat confused Peng at our side, we started walking through Chinatown, stopping at Chinese restaurants, even knocking on the doors of those restaurants that had closed for the night, asking if anyone there could translate his dialect. We must have stopped into twenty-five or thirty restaurants, and we received a wide range of reactions from the wait staff and other restaurant workers, many of whom were suspicious about this unorthodox crew approaching them. They must have thought, *Who are these people, and why are they asking us questions?* Some of them probably had their own very good reasons not to talk to just anyone.

Finally, after nearly an hour of traipsing through Chinatown, we found someone who spoke and understood Peng's dialect. Realizing that we were all very hungry, we invited him out to dinner with our group so he could translate for us while we ate a meal. Laurie remembers a lot of details about that unforgettable late afternoon and evening. "I'd ask people in Mandarin if they knew that dialect, and when we found a man who did, we were so relieved," she says. "I know I was relieved for Peng because I felt so bad that he had to deal with speaking in a language he didn't know very well and speaking to me, a person whose Mandarin was far from perfect. I knew it would be a source of comfort to have someone he could openly speak with."

It turns out that Peng had never eaten in a restaurant before or even been inside one, which was one of many firsts he experienced that day and would continue to experience. He found it hard to believe that he could order anything on the menu and looked around the restaurant and then back to us shaking his head in utter amazement. He didn't know what he wanted to eat, so we decided to go big—after all, this was a spontaneous celebration of Peng's new-found freedom—so with Laurie's help we ordered heaping plates of various meat, chicken, seafood, and vegetable rice and noodle dishes. Although Peng seemed bewildered by the entire experience, when the food arrived at our table he dug in, demonstrating just how hungry he was.

Through the translator, we were able to explain to Peng that we were going to put him up in a hotel that night, another first-ever experience for him. Laurie would pick him up in the morning and bring him to my office to talk about our plans moving forward. We'd buy him food and provisions to tide him over, and a new bus ticket, and then send him on his way to stay with his uncle in upstate New York.

After dinner, Laurie walked Peng to the hotel, again watching his eyes widen and his head turn in every direction as he took in all the sights and sounds of Boston at night. She also made sure that he understood that he needed to be ready when she came back the next morning. "I talked to Peng that night at the hotel, telling him over and over that I'd be back at such-and-such a time in the morning to take him to Susan's office," she recalls. "I also had the front desk call at a certain time. When I returned to the hotel in the morning to pick him up, he was sitting there all ready to go. Although Peng was sometimes hard to read, he was always very reliable in the end. And as we got to know each other, we became closer with him, learning many things, including what a loving, dedicated father he was."

When Laurie helped Peng check out the next day, she got quite a surprise at the hotel's front desk. "He didn't know how to activate the TV remote, so when I got the bill, there was something like $200 in movie rentals," she says. "He must have turned the TV on and then just started pressing buttons, unintentionally ordering movie after movie. Later, Susan asked me to contact the hotel clerks, to explain the situation and ask to get the charges removed, which they did."

The next day, in my office, we explained to Peng, as best we could, that it would be critical for us to be able to stay in close contact with him and that he would need to come back to Boston for his first hearing in late November. We told him he'd need to arrive early so we could prepare him carefully for the hearing and the next steps in his case.

Fortunately, he still had his uncle's phone number on the same scrap of paper that miraculously survived his Burmese mountain climb and every other obstacle he had faced in his trek to the United States. We called his uncle at his Chinese restaurant to talk, and although he didn't speak much English or Mandarin, he put a nice young woman on the phone, and she served as a translator. We explained who we were, that we had Peng with us, and that we would be helping him on a pro bono basis to try to secure asylum for him.

"We also need to stay in constant communication with you and Peng," I told the uncle. "We need your help in arranging for Peng to return to Boston every time we have a hearing. And please, please, please meet him at the bus station when he arrives this afternoon."

I hoped our urgings were getting through, but I couldn't help but worry, saying to myself, "Please, Lord, don't let us lose him again."

Laurie experienced the same sort of anxiety. "Susan and I were so concerned about whether the uncle would be there at the right time," Laurie says, "and if he understood the importance of staying in contact with us. It was unnerving, but we had no other choice, and his uncle was very helpful all along the way and helped make sure Peng arrived in plenty of time before each hearing."

Performing the Legal Heavy Lifting

The first hearing went as I expected. I did not contest that Peng was deportable—after all, he did enter the United States without valid documents, which is typical for those fleeing persecution. They usually are running for their lives, and many can't afford the luxury of applying for a passport. But I stated that he had a defense to deportation—namely, his valid claim to political asylum.

The court then set the hearing schedule for the asylum case and assigned the case to an immigration judge, who would preside over the asylum hearing and make the ultimate decision. I'm always on edge during this nerve-racking moment, because all judges bring to the court-room different approaches to their dockets, interpretations of the law, personalities, and attitudes. Some are professional and kind; others aren't, but they're fair; one or two are horrible, notorious for the way they mis-treat people. As I waited to hear who would be assigned to Peng's case, I felt that familiar tightness in my chest.

I remember thinking, *Who will it be? Who are we getting? Please, not the aggressive, erratic, and often unstable and unprofessional immigration judge. Not the one I'd seen and heard on several occasions yelling at the immigrants in his courtroom, sometimes making them cry. Not the one who always elicited in me a deep sense of sadness that the system had seen fit to elevate this clearly unqualified individual to such a weighty position. Please, not THAT judge.*

Unfortunately for Peng, and for me, we learned the notorious judge would preside over Peng's case. We drew the short straw, and it was a frightening prospect.

My legal team and I had our work cut out for us. While the case took many twists and turns and sometimes required creative legal maneuver-ing, I won't go into great detail about all the litigation preparation and strategic executions. I will say that—to win this case and gain Peng polit-ical asylum so he could bring his family to the United States and start a new life together—we worked meticulously to collect a huge amount of evidence, including working with Peng and his uncle to contact people from his village who could corroborate what happened. That wasn't easy, because, like Peng, many of them were illiterate, as well as hard to track down in that rural province in southern China. We had to make several long-distance phone calls, which took many tries before we connected with the right people.

I knew we needed to get statements from neighbors in the village who had witnessed what had happened to Peng and his family and find out how his wife and their newborn third child were doing. One day, while Peng, my team, and I were sitting in our conference room making international calls to China and gathering information, we received tragic news. The authorities had found his wife—pregnant with their third child—apprehended her, and ordered doctors to conduct a horrendous eighth-month forced abortion. Peng had believed all along that his wife had delivered the baby. Instead, he learned that she became seriously ill and nearly died from the extremely dangerous procedure. He sat there stunned. It was a terrible blow to him and heartbreaking for us to witness him learning this.

After hearing that awful news, we knew it was more imperative than ever to continue to build the strongest case we could, win asylum for Peng, and reunite his family here in the United States.

To that end, we sought out the leading experts on China's one-child policy to provide testimony in the case, including a former INS general counsel, Grover Joseph Rees. While reaching out to such a lofty individual to serve as an expert witness might have seemed a bit over the top, I needed Joseph and the weight of his position to prove what the correct legal standard should be in Peng's case, as the standard for asylum cases based on failure to follow China's coercive family planning policies had undergone several shifts in the years leading up to Peng's case. The INS in Peng's case was clearly applying the wrong standard, one that had been superseded by law. I also presented the written and telephonic testimony of Professor David Zweig, one of the foremost academic scholars and experts on China. He was teaching at a university in Hong Kong at the time and testified by phone. Finally, I presented testimony from John Aird, a prominent social scientist and the leading expert in the United States on China's one-child policy.

The judge demonstrated his infamous erratic behavior and questionable decision-making a few times during the course of the four-year political asylum trial in Boston Immigration Court. That's right, it took *four years* to present our case! The judge limited our hearings to short sessions, never long enough to put forward all of our voluminous evidence, forcing us into a stop-and-start hearing process. I'd requested full eight-hour hearing slots, rather than the typical three- to four-hour sessions, a request that's often honored, provided that there's good cause. We had very good cause, because we had gathered a mountain of evidence to submit to prove Peng's case, including the detailed testimony of so many experts, and we needed the eight-hour timeframes. Peng would return to Boston for a three- to four-hour hearing, which the judge would then continue eight or nine months later—or longer. The entire process was conducted in an inefficient and piecemeal fashion, requiring us to prepare and get back up to speed on the case in hearings that spanned from November 1993 until December 1997.

Over the course of those four years, the hearings took on a very adversarial dynamic, fraught with acrimony and fiercely competitive—a pitched battle, I would say. It was never at all certain that we would actually win, judging from the extreme opposition from the INS trial attorneys who were assigned to the case. They threw every hook and jab they had at us, sometimes with strategic strikes, sometimes wildly flailing, doing all they could to land a knockout punch.

But . . .

We won! The judge ruled in Peng's favor in December 1997, five long years after I took on the case. Naturally, I was jubilant. With most clients, I would have immediately picked up the phone to tell them the great news, but it was still hard to communicate with Peng. So, the same day we received the judge's decision, I sent him a short but sweet letter, letting him know his asylum ordeal was over and that we would continue to represent him to file for a green card one year later (a one-year waiting period was required) and would work to reunite his family with him. While we couldn't talk about this victory, I knew in my heart that Peng would be relieved beyond measure. I also reached out to share the news with Laurie. While many people had worked on Peng's case after Laurie's two-year stint at the firm had ended and she'd gone on to pursue her successful legal and educational careers, I would never think about his case without thinking of her. And, of course, Laurie was elated to hear the good news.

It took quite some time after that to secure Peng's permanent residence, or green card, status and to process the applications for his family members to join him as derivative asylees. This allows immediate family members to get the same kind of immigration status and benefit at a U.S. consulate overseas that the asylum winner received inside the U.S.

We processed the cases for Peng and his family members for a running period of fourteen years, and I brought in many different lawyers and assistants to help achieve all these results during that time span. It truly was a team effort.

To this day, I remember Peng's case as one of the most dramatic in my career, especially because we came so close to losing him into the vastness of the United States the day he was released from detention. I'll never forget the horrors he, his wife, and his family suffered at the hands of the Chinese government and that his wife almost didn't survive the eighth-month forced abortion. She also suffered other health conditions. "My wife was so stressed in China, and she became sick and had to rely on medications every day," Peng says.

For much of the time that he's been in the United States, Peng worked long hours in a Chinese restaurant, waiting for the day his family could join him. That finally happened on August 18, 2000, eight years after he hiked over mountains in Southeast Asia into Burma to board a boat and then onto five airplanes to reach Boston. He expresses his gratitude and joy when he "realized my dream to reunite my family" and adds simply and concisely, "With my family with me, life in America is safe and very good."

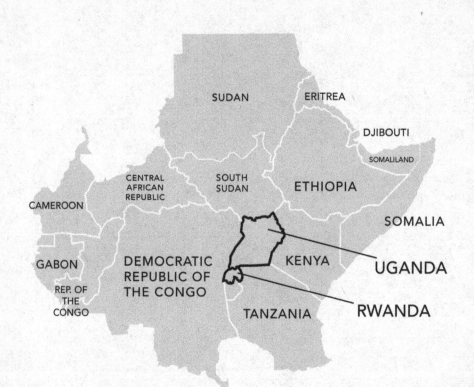

CHAPTER 8

KINDNESS INCARNATE:

ESCAPING WAR AND GENOCIDE, EAST AFRICAN WOMAN ENDURES ATROCITIES TO PROVIDE CARE TO AT-RISK CHILDREN

For years, Audrey Uwimana's young cousin would turn around abruptly, run as fast as she could, find a safe hiding spot, and cower in fear . . . all at the mere sight of a machete.

At the height of the infamous Rwandan genocide in 1994, near the Ugandan/Rwandan border, Audrey's three-year-old cousin stood by helplessly with her mother as militia members of the majority Hutu ethnic group invaded the family's home, brandishing machetes, and hacked her father to death. Audrey's uncle was one of hundreds of thousands of Tutsis, as well as many moderate Hutus, slaughtered by Hutu militiamen in a bloodbath that turned this region of Africa into a killing field, shocking the world. And yet, no country stepped in to try to stop the massacres.

While Audrey bore witness to many such atrocities committed by the militia forces—in her neighborhood, among her friends, and within her family—she was also a victim of violence herself, suffering severe physical pain and indescribable emotional anguish.

Now, years later, Audrey tries not to think back on all the brutality she experienced as a Rwandan Tutsi. But when asked about it, she shakes her head and releases a long, loud sigh. "What stands out the most is the utter disbelief," she says, her usually ebullient presence waning. "I never thought that we as Africans could do what we did to each other. When my family, friends, and I first heard about what was happening, we said to ourselves, *Oh no, no, no. It must be an exaggeration.* But when it comes into your neighborhood, and you hear your neighbor was hacked to death or that a husband hacked his wife to death because she was Tutsi and he was Hutu, you think, *Oh my goodness, this is real.*"

Audrey pauses and then adds, "It was real, but when I think back on it all, it seems so surreal. It just doesn't make any sense at all. I cannot believe that humans—and I'll put 'humans' in quotes—can be so inhuman."

While Audrey has seen and struggled through so much inhumanity— and, at one point, she was so sick her doctors thought she'd not survive—she has persevered and thrived, drawing on an innate combination of compassion and strength. Today, she volunteers for a U.S. nonprofit organization that provides comfort and care to abandoned children, epitomizing the very essence of humanity.

Rigorous yet Holistic and Egalitarian Education

Violent attacks between Hutus and Tutsis flared up in Rwanda for years, prior to the one-hundred-day period in 1994 that's commonly referred to as the *Rwandan Genocide,* and Audrey's family was not spared. One of twelve children, Audrey was six years old when her grandparents were attacked and killed by extremist Hutus, a group that had long clashed with the minority Tutsis. In a harrowing attempt to survive by fleeing the violence, the family crossed into Uganda. Eventually, Audrey, her parents, siblings, and three extended family members found shelter in a refugee camp, where they would live for the next sixteen years. During that very dangerous pregenocide time period, seventeen family members shared a three-room mud hut, enduring extremely degrading and humiliating conditions. They were never referred to by their individual names; they were just called "those Tutsis."

Audrey's father worked as a farmer for a local landowner, laboring long hours and saving as much money as possible to send some of his children to school. Audrey was one of the few siblings able to attend not only primary school but a private secondary school as well. Highly intelligent, she thrived academically under the tutelage of caring educators.

"That was the best foundation my parents could have given me—an excellent, exclusive school," Audrey says, adding that the tuition was very expensive; she gained admission through a scholarship. "They could put in some of the poor kids if you showed promise, intelligence, and good character."

Embracing a holistic educational and cultural approach, the school's administrators took steps to make the school the first in Uganda to emphasize extracurricular activities in addition to rigorous academics. "We had games in school," Audrey recalls. "We played tennis, volleyball, basketball, and we had a creative dance program. The school also had a swimming pool—and that was a big deal!"

Many of the kids who attended the school, including the president's son, were the children of government leaders and other Uganda power brokers, but it was philosophically founded on the egalitarian idea that one's economic class didn't matter. "We wore a uniform so we were alike," Audrey explains. "If someone didn't tell you that that was the president's son or minister's daughter, you wouldn't know who they were. That was fantastic. And, you could be the most intelligent person in the school, but it didn't get you very far if you didn't also have character and compassion. The headmaster used to tell us that his wish is that we would all give back to the community where we came from."

The aspiration the headmaster wanted for his students planted the seed in Audrey's mind that eventually led to her life's work in community service. And some of her fellow students followed a similar career path, she found out later. The entire educational experience served as a beacon of light in the darkness and violence all around her. The kindness shown to Audrey and the knowledge and worldliness she gained in the private school influenced her profoundly and became a fundamental and essential part of her persona. Without the positive anchor of her memories of those school years, Audrey may not have survived the horrendous trauma that was to befall her.

Raped, Beaten, Stabbed

In 1990, sixteen years after Audrey's family escaped the intertribal violence in Rwanda that claimed her grandparents' lives, the Tutsis formed an organized guerilla resistance to the Hutus with the help of Uganda's National Resistance Army. By 1994, the Rwanda Patriotic Front took control in Rwanda and formed a government. Many Tutsis, including Audrey's family, finally felt safe enough to return to Rwanda and made their way back to their home country.

A few years passed. One day, Audrey's large extended family was conducting a funeral for an uncle who had been murdered by Hutus. Suddenly, several heavily armed Hutu militiamen surrounded the family and ordered them to lie on the ground. The men picked out specific female family members and raped them in front of everyone else. Then they separated out the younger women and girls, including Audrey, beat them, and forcibly dragged them into a truck that was parked about thirty yards away.

Audrey's father tried to stop the Hutus, yelling that they'd have to kill him first if they wanted to take his relatives. One of them attacked him viciously with the butt of a rifle, knocking him to the ground. When her brother tried to help their father, he was shot and killed.

The assailants identified Audrey as someone who had been vocal, speaking her opinion that Hutus who engaged in genocide against the Tutsis should be prosecuted and brought to justice. When Audrey was rounded up, a soldier shone a flashlight in her face and said, "This is the one who has been talking all the garbage about the Hutus."

In tremendous pain and shock, Audrey woke up in a Hutu encampment in the woods, where the Hutus subjected her to brutal beatings.

One day, Audrey was ordered to collect firewood with the group. Seeing an opportunity to escape, she began to run. One of her captors caught up to her, stabbed her in the thigh with his bayonet, and dragged her back to the group. The infected wound festered for about two weeks, causing Audrey intense suffering. Eventually, however, she was able to walk again, although with great pain.

Throughout her ordeal at the encampment, the Hutus attempted to brainwash the captured Tutsis, trying to convert them to sympathize with their cause.

Finding Comfort—Temporarily

Eventually, the Hutus learned of a skirmish nearby, and everyone had to break camp and quickly escape. The captors forced the girls and young women to run with them deeper into Rwanda, but Audrey saw an opening, separated from the group, and sprinted toward the Ugandan border, thinking all the time that she'd be shot in the back. Instead, she ran through the night and into the next morning until she collapsed and fell asleep.

Audrey was awakened by a kind elderly herdsman who poked her gently with a stick and asked what she was doing there. She told him what had happened, and he brought her to his wife, who bathed her—the first time in three weeks she had bathed—gave her a meal, and made up a bed for her.

The couple essentially adopted Audrey and told her she could stay with them as long as she wanted, which she did for a solid year. Living in a daze, she suffered from acute depression. But they were kind to her and understood her plight. Their daughter Winnie, who had moved to the capital, Kampala, would come and visit, and she and Audrey became very close—like sisters. And Winnie's mother became like a second mother to Audrey.

"They saved my life," Audrey says. "You live amid all the craziness and violence and hatred, and then you come upon people like them who are so compassionate, and that's what makes the craziness so unreal. They were very tender and gentle and cared so much about me."

About a year after the couple rescued Audrey and took her into their family, they were all attacked by men who looked just like the ones who had assaulted Audrey's family at the funeral. The assailants held the parents and Winnie at gunpoint and raped Audrey, and then, still with guns drawn, forced the two young women to go with them as they retreated from the family's home. An hour later, shots rang out in the distance. Audrey could see that the militiamen had shot Winnie in the face, killing her. Amid the chaos, Audrey made her escape, dashing into the woods to hide overnight.

The next day, she returned to Winnie's home to deliver the tragic news and found the parents packing up to leave. When she told them what happened to Winnie, the mother fainted and fell to the floor. Racked with guilt, Audrey was mortified, thinking she was the source of bad luck and had brought tragedy to these kind people, her second family.

Heartbroken and distraught, she left them and traveled by bus to the home of a friend of Winnie's, whom she had previously met. The friend made arrangements to help Audrey obtain a passport so she could escape to the safety of another country. The friend coordinated a meeting with a Ugandan official so Audrey could explain that, as a Rwandan Tutsi, she feared for her life and needed to escape to the United States or Great

Britain. He told her that he understood the danger and agreed that she should leave the country and flee to the United States. He offered to help her secure a Ugandan passport.

While the passport initially helped Audrey flee the country, the fact that it was a Ugandan passport and not Rwandan would later prove to be the source of a very difficult challenge for her—and, as it turned out, for me as well.

Meeting Audrey

Soon after, Audrey arrived in the United States and managed to find an attorney who filed her asylum application but failed to win her case. This ultimately placed Audrey in a defensive and precarious position, leading her into a much more protracted process than if she'd succeeded in her initial attempt to win asylum. During the initial hearing, the immigration judge—a former immigration attorney who, at times, could be very strict and stern behind the bench—found Audrey's testimony to be credible and believed her descriptions of the many violent acts committed against her and the suffering she endured. Nonetheless, the judge denied the asylum application on the sole ground that she believed Audrey was a dual citizen of both Rwanda and Uganda and that she could be safely deported back to Uganda without fear of persecution there. And that's where the Ugandan passport worked against Audrey because it seemed to indicate dual citizenship.

Eventually, I came into the picture along with my associate Jeannie Smoot after receiving the case from PAIR.

I clearly remember meeting Audrey for the first time in late 2000 and was immediately drawn to this charming, highly educated, compassionate, dignified woman. I had read about her in the case summary that PAIR had sent me, but in that first in-person meeting, she shared her life experiences in painful detail. Audrey was in very bad shape emotionally and physically, living in such a dark mental state because of what had been done to her. At that particular time, she was also suffering from a debilitating illness, which left her physically weak and very tired.

Audrey recalls the state of mind she was in then. "Because of everything that had happened to me, I was deep in the throngs of depression," she says. "I moved to the U.S. when I was already depressed but I had no idea. When you've been in it for so long, it's a part of your life. I was eventually diagnosed as clinically depressed."

While it was painful for Audrey to describe the details of her experiences, it was important for me to hear as much as she cared to tell me, and like virtually all of my clients, she opened up and let it all pour out. My heart just breaks for these people. It's kind of like an out-of-body experience when you're hearing from the client about the atrocities that happened to them. You have to separate yourself; the lawyer in me has to be very matter-of-fact about it. And you have to keep your calm to help the client stay focused and not break down or fall apart too much. I always have a box of tissues on the table for all the asylum clients, and there has never been a time when they weren't needed.

My goal is always to put my clients at ease, telling them that they have enough to deal with and don't need to worry about the legal part. "Please trust that we'll do everything we can to win your case and help you get to a place of peace at some point," I tell them.

Conducting the Legal Calculus

I was not Audrey's first immigration lawyer. By the time I met Audrey, she was already in removal (deportation) proceedings. Under certain circumstances, U.S. law gives a person a second "bite at the apple" by allowing them to renew the asylum application in deportation court proceedings before an immigration judge. Audrey's first immigration lawyer had let her down. She had high hopes of succeeding in her initial asylum claim, but her first lawyer was unhelpful and had made himself scarce. She found herself facing deportation proceedings with no lawyer to advise her. Audrey recounted to me how she wrote to the immigration judge herself, explaining that she'd been abandoned by her immigration lawyer and didn't know where to turn for help. She will never forget that the female judge wrote back to her, thanking her for taking the initiative of writing to her and pausing her case so she could find a lawyer to represent her. The judge sent her a list of nonprofit organizations. She saw PAIR on the list; PAIR reached out to me, and that's how we met. My first act as her lawyer was to appeal the judge's denial of her asylum claim to the Board of Immigration Appeals, which allowed Audrey to stay in the country to fight the wrongful denial while the appeal was pending.

I knew exactly what strategy we needed to deploy to win Audrey's case, and it centered on that Ugandan passport. We had to convince the government of the truth: that she was truly not a Ugandan citizen, despite having been issued a passport from that country. The government's position was that, even if she wasn't legally a Ugandan citizen, she'd been "firmly resettled" in Uganda and therefore had a safe place to return to upon deportation. Naturally, we disagreed and felt the facts clearly demonstrated that we were right.

My colleagues and I conducted extensive legal research to dispute any notion that Audrey was either a Ugandan citizen or had been firmly resettled in Uganda. We had to delve deeply into every aspect of Audrey's family's life as refugees from Rwanda in the Ugandan camp and draw distinctions between the rights of Ugandan citizens and the lack of rights of Rwandan refugees. We needed to show the deprivations they encountered and their inability to access basic government benefits that Ugandan citizens enjoy.

Our brief to the Board of Immigration Appeals contained twenty-five single-spaced pages of indisputable, meticulously researched legal arguments. We gathered and presented new evidence that Audrey's previous lawyer had not brought forth. Taking both a big-picture perspective and a microscopic examination of the many details, we demonstrated that it was impossible that Audrey was a Ugandan citizen. Nor had she been firmly resettled in Uganda, either during her years in the refugee camp or later, after all the atrocities she suffered during the year she spent in Uganda before escaping to the United States. And importantly, we had to emphasize that if she were deported to Rwanda, the only country in which she was a citizen, her life would be in perilous jeopardy.

Through a lot of legal maneuvering, based on the mountain of research we collected, we convinced the appeals board to send Audrey's asylum case back to the immigration judge who had ruled against her, allowing us to present the evidence and testimony.

Audrey, my team, and I were ecstatic that all our hard work had paid off, and Audrey would have another shot at winning asylum. That meant more diligent toil and long hours, but with that injection of adrenaline from the appeals board, we were up for it. We moved into high gear to prepare witnesses to testify to all the pertinent facts, line up the voluminous evidence, and be more than ready for a trial on the issues. The lengthy brief we submitted contained layers of fact after fact that offered indisputable proof of our steadfast position.

As an older attorney now, I get exhausted simply thinking back on how relentless we were in building unassailable, airtight cases for our many clients, including Audrey. But we wouldn't have it any other way.

Although we believed another hearing shouldn't be necessary, for a few reasons, most importantly because our evidence was so strong, we showed up for the first *new* hearing—nearly two years after the original one. Despite that the government lawyers declined to issue any opposition to our original motion, the same immigration judge who denied the first application gave those lawyers an additional five weeks to submit their own brief opposing our position about Audrey's lack of Ugandan citizenship. Eight weeks passed, and they never submitted any such brief, probably because our position was ironclad and our evidence irrefutable.

By that time, I'd had enough and took a chance with a move that might anger the judge but one that was a carefully calculated decision. I went all out. I filed a motion to grant asylum with the court, effectively saying we'd proved that Audrey was entitled to this status and that the government had given up on any attempt to counter our arguments. It made no sense to me to rehash all the issues in another long, drawn-out hearing when the government declined to contest our argument.

Soon after filing that motion in November 2003, I received mail from the court, which I knew held the big decision. This is always a tense, drum-roll-type moment. I nervously opened the envelope and read the great news. Our strategy worked! The same judge who originally denied Audrey's first asylum application had now approved it. Her long legal odyssey was over.

Audrey was overjoyed of course and felt a great sense of relief. Yet she was still extremely sick, as she was throughout the time we worked together. Basically penniless, she lived in a room in a house with almost no support system, traumatized by all the tragic experiences, and extremely weak from a long illness. Many of us, including her doctors, worried that she wouldn't survive long enough to witness her asylum win.

A Joyous Christmas

I offered support and friendship to Audrey when I could and, in her beautiful East African British accent, she always expressed her genuine gratitude. Although I was not much older than Audrey, I felt very motherly toward her and wanted to do everything I could to make her feel cared for and welcomed.

On a cold, snowy early December day, after meeting with Audrey in my Boston office, I took her shopping. Living in the warm tropical climate of Rwanda and Uganda all of her life, she didn't own clothes suitable for the harsh Northeast winter. I wanted to buy her a warm winter coat of her choosing. She picked out one that she really liked, and I'll always remember her ear-to-ear smile as she tried it on, as I purchased it, and especially when she proudly wore it out of the store. Walking down the frosty city streets, I also recall inviting her to travel back to Boston for a Christmas dinner because I knew she was Christian and celebrated the holiday.

Well, let me say, as a Jewish woman in a Jewish family who doesn't celebrate Christmas, I had no idea how to host this holiday celebration. Hanukah, I knew, of course. Christmas, not so much; in fact, I was comically ignorant. But, of course, I understood enough to know that Christmas trees were an important part of the merriment. But I didn't want a big tree—this was a one-shot deal, and after Audrey left, I was going to get rid of it—so I bought a little two-foot Christmas *bush*. I also bought a few red and white decorations and some gifts for Audrey. I remembered hearing that roasted goose was a classic Christmas main dish, but, instead, I went with a nice roasted chicken, potatoes, vegetables, and chocolate cake for dessert. (I didn't even look for bread pudding.) I recall looking around the house before Audrey came over, smiling and thinking, *All in all, things are looking quite . . . well . . . Christmas-y.*

I arranged for transportation so Audrey could come and visit. She looked so delighted when she entered our home, dressed in festive attire, beaming with Christmas spirit. After dinner, I gave her the gifts, which included a set of Harry Potter books. I thought the rich world of wizards that J. K. Rowling's books evoked would allow Audrey to lose herself and forget her troubles for a while. I remember, on our shopping trip, I asked Audrey if she'd heard of the books. She said, "Aren't they children's books?"

"No, they're not only for kids and young adults," I told her. "Many adults like them. You might like them too."

Years later, Audrey says that the books and the Christmas celebration brought her some much-needed respite. "The school in the Potter books reminded me of the private school I attended; I'm telling you I could not put those books down," she says with a laugh. "It was all a very pleasant Christmas experience—a joyous occasion. And that's what I needed."

Over the years, I invited Audrey to visit us at our house on a number of occasions, and I think that meant a lot to her. I know it meant a lot to my family. But perhaps no visit meant more than that Christmas.

Phoenix Rising to Perform a Magnanimous Endeavor

For quite some time, Audrey had been thinking about what she'd like to do in her postasylum life, even before we'd won her case. For a while, she worked as a nurse assistant and gained a lot of satisfaction in helping others. "It was very rewarding work," she says, adding that serving others also contributed to her healing process.

Yet she soon realized that that job, worthy as it was, was not her calling. Because she saw firsthand the tragic consequences of so many children in Africa who were orphaned because of the violence in Rwanda and Uganda, Audrey soon realized that she wanted to devote her life to helping at-risk children in her community. Once she set this goal, she began to work toward turning this dream into a reality. For many years, she has worked with a community nonprofit organization dedicated to helping vulnerable children. Spending all her days attending to her beloved adopted children has given her a new lease on life.

With her immigration trauma more than twenty years behind her, Audrey occasionally is able to return to Africa and visit old friends. And whenever she's in Africa, she acts as an international emissary of sorts. Indeed, she literally sings praises of the United States whenever she gets the chance. When asked about this, Audrey initially gets light hearted: "My favorite song is 'I'm Proud to Be an American.' I hum it all the time," she says, referring to Beyonce's song. She pauses and adds, "Wherever I go, I feel proudest to be an American. America saved my life. I wouldn't be alive if I hadn't come to the U.S."

Indeed, the United States serves as a sanctuary for this remarkable woman, who now spends so much of her time giving back to her community.

With all of the terrible things that happened to Audrey, she could have turned out to be so damaged that she'd be incapable of doing anything productive. But she rose above it all like a phoenix and decided to devote her life to helping other people. It's extraordinary to me—to come out of all that dark pain with the fortitude and will to do what she's doing today and doing it so well. She has so much inner strength and yet she's very gentle.

In contemplating the brutal genocide that pitted Rwandan Hutus and Tutsis against each other, Audrey says that she searched her conscience and asked herself, *Could I do harm to anybody?* No, she concluded, she couldn't harm another person. "I cry when I see somebody crying," she says and laughs at herself. "If somebody killed me, they might very well get the death penalty, and I don't think that would solve anything. It would just bring suffering to another family."

She adds that she dislikes the sentiment behind the expression *an eye for an eye*. "I don't believe in violence begetting violence or unhappiness begetting unhappiness. I believe in breaking that cycle. It's one of the reasons why I decided to help at-risk kids."

Audrey's biggest fear growing up was losing her parents, saying if she had, she would have "given up on life," and considers herself very fortunate to have had loving, supportive parents. "I was lucky that, when I was growing up, I had my parents. I knew the love of parents," she says. "When so many kids were left orphans after the genocide, I wondered how they could wake up every day without somebody to lead them through the day, through life. So I knew that helping children would become my life's work—to be that anchor for abandoned children."

MEXICO

BELIZE

HONDURAS

GUATEMALA

EL SALVADOR

NICARAGUA

COSTA RICA

PANAMA

CHAPTER 9

A CATALYST FOR POSITIVE CHANGE:

HONDURAN IMMIGRANT AND EDUCATOR
TRANSFORMS U.S. SCHOOL SYSTEMS

O n a summer evening in 2006, José Salgado was returning to Boston from his home country of Honduras, where he needed to get his visa stamped, enabling him to continue living and working in the United States. At a layover in Miami, he deplaned. Inside the terminal, two U.S. Customs and Border Protection (CBP) officers confronted him. Clearly suspicious of this well-dressed passenger, one of the officers snatched José's visa from his outstretched hand, scrutinized it, and stared into his eyes.

Always polite, José started to explain his reason for traveling, when the officer turned to his colleague said, "'This guy has this visa and says he's a principal in a Boston public school,'" José recalls.

Both CBP officers started peppering him with questions, likely wondering who they were dealing with, who this guy was connected with, and what were his real reasons for seeking to enter the United States. They were exerting their authority, apparently trying to intimidate him through their interrogation. "It felt like harassment to me," José recalls, years later. "I told them that I didn't understand why they didn't believe me. I pointed at my visa photo and said, 'Here I am. That's me.' I pointed to a previous stamp on my passport, and said, 'This stamp says Harvard. See? Why are you doing this? I've done nothing wrong.'"

While being detained by the customs officers, José talked to another international traveler who was also being held in custody for no apparent reason. "He said he'd been there for three hours," José says, noting that at one point the detainee stood and asked, again, why he was being held. "The officer yelled at him, 'Just sit down! NOW!' And then he looked at me and said defiantly, 'I'm the one in charge here.'"

After more than an hour of aggressive and unjustified questioning—and after José told them he didn't have to answer any more of their questions and filled out a form documenting his intimidating and unwarranted mistreatment—the officers decided he posed no danger and released him, allowing him to continue his trip back home to Boston. As well they should have. A recipient of a PhD in education from Harvard, Dr. José Salgado was truly all that he said he was and much more.

Pioneering Success

The incident in Miami, however, wasn't the first of its kind, nor would it be the last. He experienced aggressive treatment that he considered harassment both while traveling and going about his daily life. Like too many immigrants, as well as U.S. citizens who are people of color, over the years, José has suffered discrimination and has been subjected to blatant racism in the United States.

Despite these unfortunate negative experiences, José's overriding feeling about the United States is one of tremendous admiration and love of this country, the promise it holds, and the opportunities it has given him as a scholar, an extraordinary teacher and leader, and the creator of successful educational models. For thousands of people in both the United States and Honduras, the feeling is mutual. Many admire and love José and the contributions he's made and continues to make in improving students' lives and transforming education systems and institutions everywhere he goes.

While José's dynamic personality, wit, warmth, and communication skills help him gain rapport with all students, he's especially gifted at connecting with marginalized and higher-risk students. He also persuasively supports multicultural education and promotes and designs curricula to embrace other cultures' histories, texts, values, and perspectives. He speaks English, Spanish, Portuguese, and French, and he understands and uses sign language. He produces remarkable results, and people take notice.

For example, in 2006, Boston's mayor Thomas Menino enthusiastically advocated for José to stay in the U.S., hailing him as "an educator of extraordinary ability," and "a genuine pioneer" for the work he'd done as principal at Boston's Umana-Barnes Middle School and elsewhere. The mayor praised José for "achievements [that] place him at the forefront of his field of endeavor, not just in the City of Boston but increasingly wherever experts search for success stories about inner-city schools and the education of children who are at risk."

Indeed, Jeanne Umana in her remarks in October 2007 at the rededication ceremony of the Mario Umana Middle School Academy, which was renamed for her late father—a prominent and popular Massachusetts legislator and a Boston judge—said, "Dr. José Salgado has turned a school struggling to find its way into one that is a national model for other middle schools."

But equally importantly, the students themselves appreciate José for the positive impact he's had in developing their minds, opening their hearts, and enhancing their lives.

José's former students at Umana-Barnes, other schools, and at the college level often credit him for what he did for them. Here's what one student who took a college class with José—he asks students to call him by his first name—said on ratemyprofessor.com: "José's class awakened me to the true meaning of education within humanity. He is the most open and caring prof I've ever had and allows all students to address issues such as sexism, racism, etc., and how they relate to education. He facilitates critical, organic learning, and personal growth just as teachers should. He will change your life."

The Model's Dynamic Specifics

Before José's arrival, Umana-Barnes was often characterized as chaotic and was considered one of the most troubled middle schools in the nation. It teetered on the precipice of collapse. Located in one of the poorest neighborhoods in Boston, the middle school suffered serious discipline problems and each year averaged 300 incidents severe enough to be reported to the police. Students came to school hungry, with ninety percent of them qualifying for free lunch and all of them qualifying for free breakfast. Many of the students and their parents had no access to health care. Because many parents worked long hours at two full-time jobs, often students came home to empty houses and spent too much time unattended.

In the new educational model, José designed, implemented, and integrated a series of changes that altered the very fabric of the school. At the centerpiece of the overhaul were longer school days. By applying what's called the extended learning time approach, which was gaining popularity at the time, José and his staff added three hours to the middle school's day—an hour longer than what many schools that used the ELT model had added to their school days. The extra time, made possible with funding that José helped secure, allowed teachers and staff to address what

José calls the "access gap," meaning students' inability to access nutritious food, daily exercise, health care, theater, music and dance performances, and knowledge about their culture.

The new system José designed combined academics with music, visual arts, theater, and sports. Each student was given a personalized plan that encouraged and recognized their need to create. José and his team carefully customized classes in writing, spelling, and reading for all students performing four to six years below grade level. José made sure that programs such as cooking, hip hop dancing, kickboxing, and tai chi were added to the curriculum to encourage healthy eating and exercise and reduce obesity. José met with students every day so they could share their ideas and suggestions and let them know they were seen and heard. With his insightful ELT approach, José reduced truancy by seventy percent, and eighty percent of students passed their math standardized test.

And those were only some of the changes that improved students' education in many quantifiable ways. He also collaborated with social workers, the school psychologist, parents, law enforcement officials, and others as part of his holistic approach. Some of the changes even occurred at a granular level. For example, José made sure that the junk food in the vending machines was replaced with nutritious, brain-building snacks and drinks. With José as the school's architect and leader, the Umana-Barnes School did indeed become a national success story.

From Agri-Engineer to English Teacher

José grew up in a lower-middle-class neighborhood in Honduras with a very supportive family who valued the importance of education. "My parents made tremendous sacrifices to send me to a private Catholic school; they really struggled, and I'll always be grateful," he says.

As a teenager, José learned of an exchange program that might be available to him—the popular and extensive AFS Intercultural Program (originally known as the American Field Service Program). That is, if his family could afford its costly price tag. Determined to give him this experience, his parents put in extra time and effort at their jobs to raise money to send him abroad to take part in this program. "I became an exchange student in Plymouth, Wisconsin," he says. "That shaped my understanding of the United States, and I'm still very close to my host brother."

He'd never been out of Honduras, nor had he ever been on an airplane. His time in Wisconsin proved to be enlightening and valuable and allowed him to improve his English. Having grown up with American television in his home country, he'd sometimes see shows depicting farms in the U.S. heartland with their classic red barns, lush green fields dotted with grazing cows, and steel-gray silos, much like those in The Dairy State. "One thing I found really weird at that time," he says, chuckling. "When I was young, I'd see cartoons of farms in the Midwest, and then I got to Wisconsin and I thought, *Oh my god, they're real!*"

Not long after José returned home and graduated high school, he attended the National Autonomous University of Honduras and studied to be an agricultural engineer, a common career for people in Central America, earning a bachelor's degree in agricultural engineering with a specialization in genetic engineering in 1987. "I loved it," he recalls. "It was by the ocean, I had a lot of friends from the English-speaking part of Honduras, and I also taught English as a second language." While the job didn't pay much, this is where he discovered his passion for what he wanted to do for a living. "I knew then that I wanted to pursue a career in education," he says.

Soon, José applied for a Fulbright scholarship and had to pass the interview stage of the application process. "At the interview," he says, "one of the questions was 'Why would you want to teach English when you're an engineer?' My response was 'Because Honduras needs everything.

Everything.' I know for sure that that helped me get the scholarship, because everybody in the room nodded yes."

As a result of attaining the Fulbright, José traveled to Massachusetts on an exchange visitor visa to earn a master's degree in international education at the Boston University School of Education. Here, he took classes from some of the best American minds in their respective fields, including the famous author and scholar Elie Wiesel and Bruce Fraser, a pioneer in linguistics and education.

José felt incredibly comfortable in this higher-education setting and thrived academically: "I thought, *This is it. I am home.* I excelled in ways that I had no idea a human could excel in. I had great professors who changed the way I thought. They wanted students to offer their analysis. My mind was bubbling. I had no idea that there was this intellectual world in the United States. It had not just financial wealth but intellectual wealth—and intellectual freedom. I read books I was not allowed to read in Honduras. I could express my ideas, which are considered leftist by some. For example, that it's simply not acceptable that the Honduras militia could kill children in the street and the homeless and homosexuals and people who expressed any sort of opposition to the government."

He also felt right at home—safe and secure—with his new living environment. "When I came to Boston," he says, "the biggest thrill for me was to walk around my neighborhood in the summer at 2:00 in the morning because I knew nothing was going to happen to me. You can't do that in Honduras."

Certainly, a lot could happen to him in the middle of the night in his home country. Much of Honduras was and continues to be dangerous for its citizens, especially those who actively seek to change and improve its established institutions and systems, many of which are reportedly corrupt. Police and security forces routinely crack down on public protests with violence and even lethal force. Violent crime runs rampant in virtually every population center, and the country's homicide rate ranks as one of the highest of any nation on the planet.

Educating the Educators at Harvard

While pursuing his graduate degree at Boston University, which he received in 1994, José conducted research into many areas of education. While much of what he learned would later inform his work as an educator, one particular realization stood out. He felt that Latino schoolchildren and children from marginalized communities in the United States were not getting the level of education that would later enable them to succeed in their new country. Today, he says that insight served as motivation to continue his education and ultimately do all he could to ensure quality education for all people, reduce dropout rates among underserved students, and increase their enrollment in postsecondary education. "I made all of that my [collective] goal and felt that if I worked hard enough, I could make a difference," he says.

So José took his education to the next level, continuing his academic pursuits by attending Harvard University, where he earned his doctorate in education policy and analysis (through its EPA Program). His professors quickly learned of José's passion for and understanding of the issues underserved students encountered and identified him as someone with both the intellectual and practical capacity to lead others. During the summer after his first year at Harvard, he was appointed to codirect the summer component of the Teacher Education Program, which launched his efforts at teaching the teachers.

The members of the School of Education liked what they saw that summer and chose José to lead the prestigious institution's Teacher Education Program, a role he performed for four years. It was virtually unheard of at Harvard to have a student take the helm of training educators, a testament to José's obvious skills and the confidence the Education Department placed in him. In addition, he also served as a graduate school lecturer and designed and taught a course called "External Influences in the Educational Systems of the Third World" and other courses with curricula centered on Latin America. His culturally sensitive courses drew educational connections between the United States and the developing world as well as immigrants to the United States.

After earning his doctorate, José served as the dean of curriculum and programs for the City of Cambridge (Massachusetts) Public Schools, where he expanded and enhanced the courses and trained teachers in innovative and effective educational methods. His service caught the attention of the community, and, in 1999, he was honored with the City of Cambridge Peace and Justice Award.

In 2004, he accepted the position of principal at Umana-Barnes and embarked on his tireless and successful efforts to transform the school.

A Mad Scramble

I met José in the summer of 2006, when he was facing an immigration crisis. After fifteen years of living legally in the United States, his visa validity period was closing very soon. I saw the worry in his eyes—and I also heard the passion in his voice when he talked about the transformative work he was doing at the Umana-Barnes Middle School. He felt an obligation to the students, teachers, and staff; they all looked to him for the leadership he demonstrated every day in helping them make great strides in the classroom. The Boston Public School system was equally stressed out about José's visa predicament.

The visa he was on, called a J-1, required him to return to Honduras for two years before he could change to a different type of work visa. Because José was subject to this requirement, it severely limited the kinds of visas he could get to legally remain here.

He told me he was more than willing to go back to Honduras for two years but not then, when he still had progress to make in improving the middle school. He needed to finish the job he started and make sure the school was firmly established as a true educational success. He wasn't alone in this desire. The school was also an extremely high priority for Boston and, indeed, for the Commonwealth of Massachusetts, including the governor, Boston's mayor, the Boston superintendent of schools, and other important stakeholders. They were very clear that they wanted and needed to keep José in Boston so he could continue his transformative work.

The only kind of visa he'd be able to get at that time, to temporarily put off the need to return to Honduras for at least two years, was a very hard visa to get—an O-1, the extraordinary ability visa.

José was not sure if he was O-1 material, but I was quite confident that he was. Like with many of my clients, my team and I faced a very tight deadline and had to race frantically to prepare and file his case before the summer came to a close. José needed to secure the visa at least by the start of the school year; the law required that. We scrambled to put the petition together quickly, and in addition to the primary evidence of José's accomplishments, we also received powerful supporting letters of recommendation from prominent Boston community leaders to present a persuasive case. I remember that one recommender, a well-regarded education leader, characterized José's accomplishment at Umana-Barnes as a "near-miraculous transformation." Another called his work "astonishing" and "unprecedented." The praise—which included very specific examples of his efforts, intelligence, and character—was truly impressive. *This educator has a rare gift,* I thought, *and when they see what he has accomplished, I think the immigration service will agree.*

Working frantically, with little time left before the start of the new school year, my team and I managed to assemble the evidence quickly and file the petition. Remarkably, it was approved in three days—no questions asked—a rare fast turnaround. With his visa in hand, José needed to return to Honduras to get the visa stamp in his passport and then come back to the States with the new visa, which he did but not without that troubling and harassing encounter with customs officers in Miami, when they unnecessarily detained him. Still, he made the long round-trip journey, returning just in time to get back to work for the Boston Public School system, where he'd be legally positioned until 2010, when he'd have to take further steps.

Despite the frenetic pace with which we had to pull everything together, José's case was fairly straightforward. I didn't worry that we wouldn't win approval, given his stellar history of contributions to the advancement of students and teachers in several settings and the letters of support and other evidence. But that doesn't mean José didn't worry. He lived every day with high anxiety hanging over him, not knowing how long he'd be able to stay in the United States, which of course took an emotional toll.

When asked about whether it was difficult living with such stress, José says, "Oh my god, yes! Absolutely." He pauses, as if trying to decide which story of many to tell, and then continues. "There are days that are harder than others. For example, in 2007, I'm in Puerto Rico taking a vacation, and I'm getting on the plane to fly back to the States when this border security guy totally comes into my space. He says, 'Where are you from?' Now, I'm completely rattled. I show him my visa. But he and another officer completely get into my face, ask questions, and demand answers. It was one of many times I was harassed—and I always act respectfully, dress nicely when I travel, and try to present myself as a professional."

Immigration attorneys understand that, while the case before us might not be the most difficult to navigate, our clients can never relax about their immigration cases: Most people pursuing an immigration application or process feel persistent anxiety about the risk of denial and the possibility of experiencing the kind of intimidating confrontation José encountered. Often, they suffer severe angst. Like so many immigration lawyers, I can't help but empathize with what my clients are going through emotionally. When I'm confident I have an approvable case, I don't worry as much about the legal outcome as I do about my clients' visceral fear of being deported or being required to leave this country. I feel it's part of my job to try to calm my clients and diminish their anxiety.

Contributing to Honduras

In 2010, José moved back to Honduras to fulfill the two-year visa requirement, but he ended up staying much longer, because he truly wanted to give back to his home country; after all, as he mentioned in his Fulbright interview, Honduras needs everything. He worked in education institutions and served in the provost role at the Technological University of Honduras. He brought many of the ideas about and approaches to education that he learned in the United States, and many of the teachers he'd talk to in Honduras were receptive to hearing about innovative models.

"I'd tell them about possibilities," he says, "and they'd say, 'Please tell me more.' I'd spend days going to schools and saying, 'Let's think about learning.' We'd do exercises and they'd say, 'Oh, I get it.' I'd demonstrate new ways to read or write." He stops for a moment and adds, "I think I planted a lot of seeds in many schools in Honduras."

Among the many "seeds" that José thinks sprouted within the minds of Honduran teachers was one of his guiding principles in educating students: Teach students how to think and how to learn and work hard to inspire them to love learning.

Eventually, José secured a work visa and made his way back to Boston. He worked a few jobs, including in an important position at Salem State University, a college north of Boston, where he taught classes as an associate professor and served as the director of the Advanced Graduate Studies program in the School of Education. Not surprisingly, he was awarded the university's Outstanding Teacher of the Year . . . twice.

Once, while lost in thought on a commuter train heading to Salem State, he heard a familiar voice, which shook him out of his ruminations. "All of a sudden, I hear someone yelling, 'José, José!'" he recalls. "I looked up and saw a former student. She told me that she wanted to thank me for something, and I asked her for what and then she said, 'You taught me how to write. Thank you, José.'"

The woman expressed her sincere appreciation for the approach he took in instructing her and her fellow students. "I told my students, among many other things, to 'write about your feelings,'" he says. "'Write about what you love. Don't worry if it flows. Just release your thoughts, and then we'll go over it together.'"

She explained that she had a daughter who died at three months old and that she was writing a book about the experience, applying the methods that José taught her. "She said she was telling that story in the way that I taught her how to write," he says, adding that she was also an educator. "She said, 'Now I'm going to teach soon-to-be teachers and principals.' Let me tell you, I was high!" He pauses and adds, "And that's what it's all about. At the end of the day, it's really not about literature or history or math. It's about relationships—with other people and to the space you're in right now."

That fleeting, en route exchange generated a synergistic effect: The student interacted with him, he interacted with her, and they each came away from that encounter with renewed passion for what they were doing with their respective lives.

In the National Interest

In 2019, José decided that the time had come to try to get a green card so he could stay in the United States permanently. He reached out to me again for help. My team and I decided he'd likely qualify for a national interest waiver green card, which is limited to those who can convince the immigration service that their work is in the national interest of the United States. We thought he'd have a strong NIW case because his work so clearly benefits U.S. education, especially for the economically disadvantaged and students of color and because of his proven ability to improve educators' teaching methods, instructing them in how to adapt components of the curricula to focus on multicultural education. We also believed we could show the government that José's reach of influence extends far beyond the education districts in which he has worked. Many of the other educators he's taught have fanned out across the country to other school systems, taking innovative ideas with them and leaving a big footprint of his impact.

We gathered voluminous evidence and letters of support to generate what we confidently felt was an irrefutable case that José serves the national interest of this nation. In fact, I consider him a national treasure. We filed his case in July 2019 . . . and waited.

José and our Mintz team anxiously waited to hear the government's answer on the first part of his case, the petition seeking approval of the national interest waiver. When we did, eleven months later, we were delighted that his petition was approved, no questions asked. His contributions were so overwhelming that the government offered no pushback whatsoever—something that rarely happens. But the second part of his case, the actual green card application, was still pending. Finally, after what seemed like interminable delays created by the COVID-19 pandemic, José received his green card. After *thirty years* from when he first arrived in the United States, he has finally secured a permanent status here and no longer has to face the immigration insecurity he felt for so long.

"The immigration uncertainty ran my life," he says. "For example, I've always been a very careful driver, and I was even more careful because I didn't want to get a ticket; anything can be used against you. I only stopped being worried about my immigration status on March 18, 2021, the day I was sure I was going to get a green card, which I received on the twenty-ninth."

Occasionally, he hears from former students. Several of them who "were kids who lived in the projects," he says, are now social workers. They often mention the compassion and interest José showed them and say they want to extend that kind of support to others in need.

Of course, others take different career paths. "I talked to a former student who is Salvadoran," he says. "I'm very proud of him. He thanked me because we provided him with a very good education at the Amigos School in Boston," he says, referring to another institution in which he taught, led by example, and transformed. "He's now an engineer for Apple in Sacramento. He's got a great job and is happily married to a wonderful woman." José takes a moment and finishes his thought, "I'm just so proud."

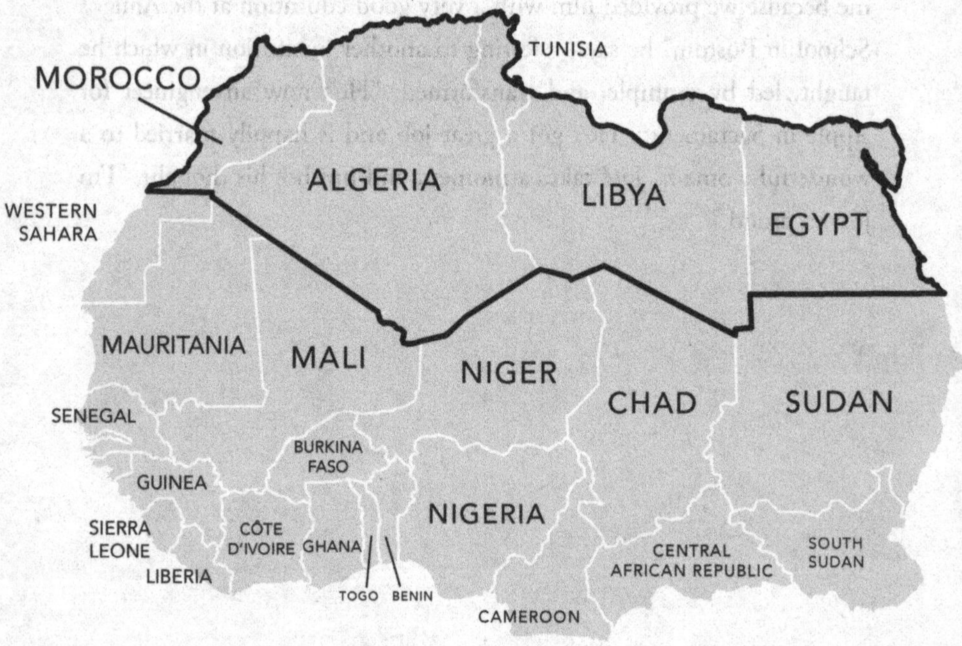
MOROCCO
TUNISIA
ALGERIA
LIBYA
EGYPT
WESTERN SAHARA
MAURITANIA
MALI
NIGER
CHAD
SUDAN
SENEGAL
BURKINA FASO
GUINEA
SIERRA LEONE
CÔTE D'IVOIRE
GHANA
NIGERIA
LIBERIA
TOGO
BENIN
CENTRAL AFRICAN REPUBLIC
SOUTH SUDAN
CAMEROON

CHAPTER 10

A STUDY IN STRENGTH, SMARTS, AND PERSISTENCE:

NORTH AFRICAN WOMAN ESCAPES DANGER, ENDURES INCOMPETENCE TO EARN CITIZENSHIP

On a warm, muggy day in early August 2019, North African–born Mariem Ayari stood with many others before a judge in a courthouse in a U.S. East Coast city, eager to take the last step in her long, difficult, and, at times, traumatic and dangerous journey to become a naturalized U.S. citizen.

Mariem vividly remembers reciting the Naturalization Oath of Allegiance to the United States of America and the feelings that monumental act evoked within her. "The judge asked us to raise our right hands, we took the oath, and then . . . I was finally an American citizen!" Mariem says, adding that it was one of the happiest, most exciting days of her life. While she exudes elation in talking about this experience, Mariem also recalls the immense relief she felt, because the reality is her citizenship nearly didn't materialize, and, in fact, her green card status could easily have been stripped away from her.

The smooth and simple proceedings on that joyful summer day stood in stark contrast to her naturalization interview only a few months before. In that setting, inside a nondescript government building, she sat alone in a sterile room with a fierce and cruel immigration officer who turned what should have been a pro forma proceeding into an abusive interrogation.

That verbally brutal encounter hit her hard emotionally, plunging Mariem back into the state of despair from which she had only recently emerged. It triggered a mental replay of the many distressing events that had plagued this brilliant, beautiful, talented, and compassionate young woman.

The aggressive inquisition brought back the trauma of living with a father who abused both her and her mother; the treatment by the American man she married, who turned out to be a con artist and, worse, a violent fiend; the racial, gender, and geographic discrimination she and many foreign-born people endure all too frequently; the carelessness of the U.S. immigration system and gross incompetence of several of her lawyers; the unwanted and highly inappropriate advances by one of her attorneys; and the underlying fear of deportation to the country that her abusive father had moved back to, compounded by the very real prospect of having to live with or near him.

And yet, Mariem's inner strength and tenacity helped her push through, and now she holds a managerial position with a high-tech company, receiving regular promotions for her stellar performance as she advances her career while helping others.

Amid Repressive Regime, Academic Excellence

Born in North Africa, Mariem, her parents, and siblings experienced plenty of ups and more than a fair share of downs. During the 1990s, her home country's authoritarian government ruled with a heavy hand and kept any form of dissent in check. In search of a calmer environment in which to live, her family relocated to the Middle East, where Mariem and her mother received a temporary residence permit.

Still, for the most part, Mariem grew up living a comfortable life despite domestic conflicts and, ultimately, her parents' divorce. "I didn't come from a poor environment," she says. "There were years when my parents struggled financially a little bit, but we were not poor. My parents, however, went through a very messy divorce."

Through it all, Mariem shined in school, receiving many academic honors and earning entry into one of the most highly regarded and academically rigorous universities in Europe. There, she earned a bachelor's degree, with high marks. She speaks four languages fluently, Arabic, French, English, and Portuguese, and can also converse in German and Greek—one of the many ways her intelligence manifests.

In 2010, Mariem moved to the Midwest to enroll in a premaster's program, where she excelled and then went on to pursue graduate studies at a northeastern university where she also worked a job on campus, volunteered in her community, and adopted a cat from a local animal shelter. Typical of her ambitious and high-achieving nature, she earned two master's degrees—an MBA and a master's degree in science, operations, and management.

The Big Con: Deceptive Romance, Thievery, and Domestic Violence

While studying at this university, Mariem met and dated Gordon, a charismatic and charming man who wined and dined her at her favorite restaurants. The romance deepened quickly—perhaps too quickly, as it turned out—and she soon moved in with Gordon. In February 2012, less than a year after they met, Gordon asked Mariem to marry him, and, one month later, they pledged their wedding vows before a legal official in a local courthouse, with the hopes of saving money for a larger wedding after Mariem's graduation. To their friends—and to Mariem—it appeared the couple couldn't be any happier.

And then Gordon began showing his true colors; his dark side started to surface.

Soon after they married, Gordon pushed Mariem to file for a green card based on their marriage. She could have waited to file without using marriage as a basis for her green card, but he kept badgering her, and, finally, she relented, essentially saying, "Okay, enough already. Fine. I'll do it." So, he petitioned for a green card on her behalf, and officials scheduled an immigration interview for the following year.

In another move in what was clearly premeditated con artistry, Gordon then started using the petition as leverage over her. Frankly and sadly, this type of immigration blackmail happens more frequently than one might think; abusive U.S. citizens, usually men, too often use their victims' immigration status as an exploitation and control device. As a master at manipulation, Gordon told Mariem that, to prove to immigration officials that they were married and truly committed to living their lives together, they needed to commingle their assets. He pleaded with her to open a joint bank account, to which she tentatively agreed. It didn't take long for Gordon to dip into the combined finances, withdrawing enough money to buy himself a car, without even checking with Mariem first.

It's important to note that it doesn't matter how intelligent, mature, and guarded a person may be—and Mariem clearly possesses these traits—a polished con artist can hoodwink virtually anybody to execute his devious deeds.

Marital and financial discord grew and grew, with Gordon coercing her to do the cooking, cleaning, laundry, and to pay the bills. Hoping to make the marriage work, Mariem initially acquiesced, performing the household duties and covering the rent and other expenses for the first several months.

"But then I told my ex that I wasn't going to let him financially abuse me anymore," she recalls. "That was his biggest problem: I was starting to resist because I was fed up."

Soon, Evil Gordon truly began to materialize. He isolated Mariem, humiliated her in front of his friends, made increasingly difficult and paranoid demands of her, and, she suspected, inflicted harm upon her cat. He abused Mariem, cheated on her openly, and hurled racist slurs at her. He forced her to perform sexual acts and take explicit photos of herself.

"He used everything against me, including where I was from," she says. "And he used me."

When Mariem resisted his demands and objected to his behavior, he threatened to withdraw his immigration petition. Her U.S. student visa status was set to expire, and, at Gordon's request—supposedly so she could focus on her green card application—she didn't apply for an extension of student status, which allows recent graduates to work in the United States to gain practical experience in their occupational field.

Gordon also threatened to lie to USCIS and say the marriage was a fraud, telling Mariem that immigration would detain her and then deport her. He told her, "If you don't take care of me, immigration will take care of you." Moreover, Gordon had encouraged Mariem to allow her visa status in the Middle Eastern country where she had lived with her mother to expire. As a result, Mariem was forced to choose between staying with Gordon and returning to the North African country and her abusive father.

She knew she had to leave him and wanted to for a long time but felt trapped because of the power he held over her regarding her immigration situation. "The immigration system is so broken, because it makes people too dependent on others," she says. "It often jails us to the people who, at one time, we chose to be with even if we no longer want to be with them. It's very difficult to leave when you want to or have to."

The clock was ticking. With one month remaining on her student visa status, Mariem was left with few options. Then, one day after a heated argument about Gordon's stubborn unwillingness to contribute any money for monthly bills, making Mariem pay them all, Gordon threatened her at gunpoint.

"He calmly told me, 'If I shoot you and you die, it would be considered an accident,'" she says.

Mariem, terrified for her life, ran out of the house, and secured a restraining order against Gordon. Soon thereafter, she learned, not surprisingly, that Gordon had withdrawn his application for her green card. Meanwhile, upon commencement from graduate school, Mariem's student visa expired, and USCIS sent her a notice that it was moving forward with removal proceedings—meaning she could very well be deported, with nowhere to go but back to North Africa.

An Avenue to Citizenship Delayed by Inappropriate Advances and Legal Incompetence

Fortunately, Congress passed the Violence Against Women Act (VAWA) in 1994, which created many protections and courses of action for female victims of violence. A provision in the legislation offers avenues to permanent residence and citizenship to certain victims of "battery or extreme cruelty committed by a U.S. citizen spouse or former spouse," according to USCIS, under its guidelines for obtaining a green card for a self-petitioner. Put another way, because Mariem was a victim of domestic violence by her American husband, the law offers a key to release the lock that Gordon used to trap her and hold her immigration status hostage.

But unlocking the pathway to obtaining VAWA-based green cards doesn't come easily because of the extensive evidentiary burden placed on VAWA petitions. Mariem—who did much of the hard work on the case herself—and her immigration attorney collected several witness accounts, including from friends of hers and Gordon's who testified about the abuse. A strong and persuasive writer who had already mentally chronicled abusive events, Mariem also drafted her own affidavit, a sixteen-page detailed account of her relationship, and she underwent an examination to prove she genuinely suffered from posttraumatic stress disorder (PTSD).

Building on the small mountain of evidence, she provided bank statements, insurance information, and copies of her leases, bills, degrees, and transcripts. The requirements also called for her to include her marriage license, Gordon's biographical information, the restraining order, extensive photos and text messages showing Gordon's multiple affairs, the divorce application, and a background check on Gordon, in which she discovered something very telling about him: He had a prior criminal history.

"I knew he had a pattern of lying and deceiving; I saw that for myself, but I never knew about [the criminal background]," she says, adding that she also learned he has a history of domestic violence.

Finally, to complete the affidavit, Mariem provided proof of volunteering activities and other facts to show "good moral character," a statutory requirement.

It seemed she had dotted and crossed all the proverbial *i*s and *t*s in lining up a strong case for herself that would still require the help of her male attorney. Unfortunately, that was a problem. Like her father, her husband, and several other men she encountered in her life, he acted abhorrently toward her. He would flirt with her, and, despite her unwillingness to reciprocate—instead sending him strong signals to cease and desist—his flirtations amplified into blatantly inappropriate advances and harassment.

"Both previous attorneys acted inappropriately," Mariem says. "The second one was worse; I felt extremely uncomfortable going to his office. He spoke French and, because he knew I spoke French, he would sometimes recite poems to me in French about beauty and love." And then, with disgust in her voice, she adds, "Finally, I told him, 'I'm your daughter's age. You said it yourself.'"

It's deeply troubling that the lawyer tried to take advantage of Mariem. Sexual harassment happens in all types of work environments, but one would hope that lawyers, doctors, therapists, and other ethics-bound service professionals would act morally and appropriately, fully understand relationship boundaries, protect, and do all they can to help their clients and patients.

Not only did this attorney act lecherously and completely inappropriately toward her, he failed to provide Mariem with even the bare minimum of competent legal service. He missed deadlines, mishandled documents, and didn't adequately communicate with her. "He was very incompetent," she says. "He messed up so many times on my case. [The immigration officials] notified him that they were going to close my case, but they never gave me copies of the documents, and he didn't tell me. Then they told him they closed the case but that he could appeal. He told me that on the last day of all of this—a process that was six to eight months long. On the last day!"

When he did make deadlines, he often made mistakes he had to try to correct. "He filed incorrect forms three times," Mariem says. "Every time he had to file for something to fix what he messed up, he would say, 'That's going to be another $500.' I was lucky because I had family members who could chip in and help when I was at a point where I could no longer afford to pay for anything. And I chose not to work under the table even though that option was available to me through several people I know. But it's not right, and I certainly didn't want to give them another excuse to use against me."

After filing the self-petition for the VAWA-based green card, Mariem had had enough and fired him. "I told him, 'I can't pay you anymore. You make mistakes and then ask me for money,'" she says, while also telling him that he made her feel very uncomfortable.

It's remarkable to think about this bold move, and it says a lot about Mariem's strength of character. On the cusp of potentially winning her permanent residency and, consequently, gaining a satisfying victory against her husband-abuser—"one reason I fought so hard to stay in the U.S. was that I didn't want my ex to win"—she walked away from her attorney, risking defeat and deportation and leaving herself without the critical legal counsel she needed. Soon after that, she reached out to me.

Gaining Ground, Getting Firmly Grounded

Mariem's not one to talk about her troubles and pain with the expectations of receiving sympathy in return. And her volunteer work in helping other immigrants provided her with an empathetic and holistic perspective. "I spent a year helping refugees who had suffered through horrible experiences," she says of her time at a refugee assistance organization. "I was the only full-time volunteer teacher. I helped the Haitians because I knew French and people from the Middle East because of my Arabic. And that work helped teach me not to feel bad for myself. It was a good reminder that I'm in a much better position than a lot of people out there."

She's exactly the type of compassionate and accomplished person we want living among us as a U.S. citizen, and she was eager to obtain her green card and move a step closer to naturalized citizenship. But of course, the system often creeps along at a tortoise-like pace. The application process for her VAWA petition took two years. Later, with help from my team, Mariem applied for and received an employment authorization card to work while her petition was pending.

In June 2014, with her second immigration lawyer, she interviewed before an adjudicator for her VAWA petition, where she was asked again to recount the horrific details of her abuse.

There was a gap in time between the above events of June 2014 and when my office got involved. But deportation still loomed over her. After

Mariem's VAWA application was approved, we worked hard to advocate to the court that it should terminate Mariem's removal proceedings as she now had a completely independent basis for a green card and permanent immigration security (or so we thought). The following August, she was granted a temporary dismissal of those proceedings pending a judgment on her petition.

Finally, we got the very good news: After years of trauma and intense anxiety, Mariem received her green card. We had a joyful celebration, and I still have the photo of her holding up her green card and beaming. We all thought this horrendous chapter of Mariem's life was closed—her immigration nightmare finally behind her.

After immigration candidates have had a green card for five years, they're eligible to apply for naturalization to citizenship. Five years after Mariem received her green card, she contacted me asking to help her become a U.S. citizen. I was delighted to hear from her. She sounded great on the phone, very centered and grounded, in a positive place, productive, and the happiest I'd ever heard her, other than the day she received her green card. In the intervening years since that day, her situation had significantly improved. Her life was sailing along smoothly, and, for the previous five years, she hadn't even needed to meet with the therapist who she had relied on for so long to overcome the experiences of the abuse and domestic violence that had so badly traumatized her.

That's not to say Mariem didn't hit some bumps in the road both at work and in everyday life. "Like many foreign-born people in the U.S., I've experienced racism on the job and in the streets just living my life. People sometimes treat me poorly," she says and then quickly adds, "But I can only imagine the mistreatment that others experience. In the work setting, a woman once asked me in front of everyone in the office what a Syrian terrorist group is like, and how can I justify what a terrorist group does. I looked straight at her and calmly said, 'I can't justify what a terrorist group does because, one, I'm not from Syria, and two, I'm not a terrorist.'"

We filed her naturalization application, and the local immigration office scheduled her for an in-person interview, as it does for everyone who applies for citizenship. Typically, these interviews are intended to verify that the applicant meets all the eligibility criteria for U.S. citizenship, with questions relating to moral character and other attributes and to ensure the applicant has no criminal or terrorist-related bars to eligibility.

I carefully prepared Mariem for her interview as I prepare all my clients. In my view, it should have been a routine interview because she had no issues about which to be worried—no criminal issues, no moral character concerns. For certain clients, I would recommend that either I or one of my colleagues accompany them if a potential trouble spot might arise that would need an attorney's explanation or if we saw a vulnerability that lurks in a gray area that requires advocacy on the client's behalf. But in Mariem's case, there was no reason for anyone to go with her, because it was a black-and-white matter. She had already done all the hard work in qualifying for permanent residency, and the citizenship calculation and questions at this point should have been very straightforward.

But I never could have prepared her for what in fact happened that day.

Under Attack

On May 28, 2019, Mariem entered the interview room and immediately felt uncomfortable with the immigration officer. "She gave me disapproving looks from the minute she saw me," Mariem recalls. "As I sat in that little room, just the two of us, and waited for her to begin the interview, I wondered what I could have possibly done to antagonize the officer."

The sad fact is that Mariem already held negative, trauma-based feelings about the government building that housed this branch of USCIS, because of her experience during a previous visit, when she requested a deportation postponement. While waiting for that interview several years earlier, during which she was asked to recount the graphic details of her abuse, she found herself surrounded by people in handcuffs and leg restraints.

"Everyone around me was shackled," she recalls, "and seeing immigrants being brought into the building in shackles was terrifying to me and is an image I'll never forget. I thought to myself, *Is this something they might do to me someday?* To me, walking in that immigration building is a traumatic experience."

With that lingering in her mind, Mariem had tried her best to steel herself for the immigration interview. Once it began, however, she immediately came under attack by the immigration officer, who deployed an arsenal of unnecessary questions, stern accusations, and outright hostility. Even though officers conducting these queries are required to exhibit sensitivity and understanding, this interviewer addressed Mariem with an aggressive tone. To Mariem, this wasn't an interview; it was an interrogation. With absolutely no legal justification, the officer questioned the underlying basis of Mariem's already-approved VAWA petition, filed six years prior. She grilled Mariem about the exact chronology and the details of her abuse, the addresses of former apartments she shared with her ex-husband, and the names of the people with whom she lived. Again, with no justification, she implied that Mariem had lied about the facts of her underlying, abuse-based green card case.

Mariem had worked diligently with her therapist to put the trauma of her earlier life behind her and to try to forget the horrid details of her abuse. Now, this insensitive and aggressive officer was dredging it all back up and also making Mariem feel like her fundamental status in the United States was at risk, when all she wanted to do was become a U.S. citizen and start voting in U.S. elections. Mariem was completely retraumatized by the questioning; she was caught completely off guard by the scary tone of the officer; she struggled to remember this information and began to cry. The officer callously dismissed her, saying something like "I have this effect on people."

After her interview, Mariem called me in hysterics; I could barely understand what she was saying because she was sobbing so much. When she stopped crying enough to tell me what happened, I was absolutely livid.

Following the abuse she suffered at Gordon's hands, Mariem was clinically diagnosed with PTSD, and it had taken many years of intensive therapy to put that trauma behind her and reclaim her life. The vicious citizenship interview conducted by the callous and harsh immigration officer triggered a new wave of emotional distress in Mariem. She cried frequently. She began to have flashbacks, anxiety, and nightmares. She couldn't sleep well. She couldn't concentrate at work. Not only had her traumatic past come back to haunt her, but now all she could think about was whether the government was going to rescind her hard-won immigration status as a result of the unjustified and misguided accusations of the officer who conducted her naturalization interview.

I told Mariem that the government would have no basis to revoke her status and that it was absolutely improper for the officer to question her prior approval. I promised her I would intervene with the government if necessary but that we should wait a few weeks to see if, the horrific interview notwithstanding, she would still receive an approval notice in the mail from USCIS. Stranger things have happened. Sometimes USCIS officers are kind and friendly, and sometimes they are mean and seem to relish the imbalanced power dynamic that is on full display in an immigration interview setting. But an officer's harsh tone and an aggressive interview does not translate automatically into a denial.

As the weeks passed with no approval, Mariem wasn't the only one who was nervous. Finally, I felt I could not wait any longer. I called the head of the immigration office to tell him what had happened and to ask for an investigation into the officer who abused her position and retraumatized my client. He was horrified as well and said he would look into it right away. I also asked him to provide sensitivity training to all the immigration officers in his charge to make sure that when someone with a VAWA-based immigration background applies for another immigration benefit requiring an interview, the immigration officers conduct their interviews with the sensitivity required when interacting with someone who has been the victim of domestic violence. He told me that they would conduct such training, and I very much appreciated that he was so open to fostering a constructive and sensitive approach to these kinds of cases. Mariem was victimized by this officer, but, hopefully, no one else in similar circumstances would be.

I was surprised, however, when months passed after my phone call, and still we didn't receive the approval. Mariem was so anxious she could barely function. She contacted me all the time to see if I had heard anything yet. It reached a point where I felt that the inordinate wait had become too much of a mental health risk for Mariem, and I had to escalate this to a higher level. I had lined up a major newspaper to do a feature story on how the agency had needlessly caused her severe emotional distress. I contacted the head of the agency again and told him the story was soon going to run in the paper. The next day, we received Mariem's approval notice. My relief was so immense that I could only imagine Mariem's. At long last, on August 1, 2019, she took the oath of citizenship in that simple, mercifully mellow proceeding and became a naturalized U.S. citizen.

Mariem's case demonstrates the power that one immigration officer can hold over an immigrant. Some immigrants suffer from overly aggressive tactics used by individual officers—especially when no one else is watching, as in Mariem's interview turned inquisition. But few have the resources to hold those officers to account. If Mariem had not turned to my team and me for help, her application might still be languishing on the desk of the horrible officer who treated her so terribly and unfairly. Worse, that officer might have unlawfully initiated a green card rescission process against Mariem. Under President Trump's administration, the government was eager to strip green card holders and even naturalized citizens of their status. A future administration could do the same.

Although Mariem felt that deep sense of relief in gaining her citizenship, it took her quite some time to fully relax about her immigration status and heal from the abuse she suffered from the immigration officer and the unnecessary, anxiety-producing delay in finally approving her citizenship case.

Today, Mariem finally feels like a whole person again and a full citizen of this country. She continues to cultivate a satisfying career working as an information technology manager and analyst and enjoys a vibrant social circle. "I've been making a better life for myself," she says.

She also uses her extensive skill sets and sincere consideration for others to help those around her. When asked what's most rewarding about her job, she doesn't hesitate to answer: "What I love about my job is that I make other people's lives easier."

SUDAN

ERITREA

DJIBOUTI

SOMALILAND

CENTRAL
AFRICAN
REPUBLIC

ETHIOPIA

CAMEROON

SOUTH SUDAN

SOMALIA

UGANDA

GABON

KENYA

DEMOCRATIC
REPUBLIC OF
THE CONGO

REP. OF
THE
CONGO

RWANDA

TANZANIA

CHAPTER 11

FROM FRONT LINES OF WAR TO FRONT LINES OF THE PANDEMIC:

SUDANESE REFUGEE SURVIVES THOUSAND-MILE WALK AND OVERCOMES KAFKAESQUE NIGHTMARE

In 1987, after nearly four years of a brutal civil war in Sudan that would ultimately span nearly two decades and claim some two million lives, twenty thousand orphaned or misplaced young boys—their lives in grave danger—fled their villages in the southern region of that East African nation. To seek shelter from what's called the Second Sudanese Civil War, they walked for weeks to reach the relative safety of nearby Ethiopia. A few years later, after war erupted in Ethiopia, they were forced to return to Sudan, trudging through torrential rain, only to face violence again.

The boys then embarked on a treacherous one-thousand-mile journey to a refugee camp in Kenya—again, on foot. By some estimates, only half of the Lost Boys of Sudan, as they became known, survived the migration to Kenya, with the other half dying along the way of malnutrition, heat stroke, disease, and attacks by wild animals.

Samuel Bol is one of the survivors.

Looking back on the horrors of the war, during which his mother died, his escape from the worn-ravaged nation, and the grueling, perilous march to Kenya, Samuel recalls the collective agony. "When the civil war broke out in Sudan, we suffered so much tragedy. Many people were tortured and killed," he says . . . and pauses. "Houses were burned down. It was real chaos. And walking to Kenya—it was very, very tough, a long struggle."

Years later, as a citizen of the United States, gainfully employed, and married but geographically separated from his wife by an ocean and a continent, Samuel engaged in a different kind of "long struggle," a bureaucratic nightmare right out of a Kafka novel. This was a painful and frustrating fiasco. It was wrapped in layers of red tape and fraught with a string of government errors and delays, absurd confusion, carelessly misplaced DNA test results, an unfortunate case of mistaken identity, and an act of spousal revenge.

"Committed to Life"

In 1992, Samuel and the other Lost Boys arrived at the refugee camp in Kenya. Most of them lived there for nearly a decade in what would grow during that time to become a sprawling but crowded city of three encampments constructed between two dry riverbeds atop the wicked-hot floor of the desert-savannah in the northwest corner of the nation. Images from aerial photography depict a sea of the dwellings packed sardine-like with half—the better half—built of wood, cane, and mud bricks. The poorer other half consisted of cobbled-together thatched roof huts, adobe mud shanties, and tents crafted of scavenged canvas. Several relief organizations operated the camp, which, at one point, included some sixty-five thousand refugees who had escaped tyranny and danger in Somalia, Ethiopia, Sudan, and Uganda.

Obviously, the conditions of the camp were extremely difficult. The United Nations High Commissioner for Refugees described the encampments as "a forlorn agglomeration at the best of times" in an evaluation report in 2000. But Samuel credits the camp's caring and dedicated relief workers with creating an environment that nurtured the boys, physically, mentally, and emotionally.

"They trained us and provided us with food and medicine," he recalls today from his home in the Northeast. "We learned a lot and got used to this way of survival. Aid workers and the community of refugees worked together to lead me and the other kids. It was easy for many of us to get tired of life. You need people to keep you motivated. You need a role model, somebody to motivate you." The teachers of the schools in Kakuma helped give him the leadership, mentoring, and structure he says he needed.

That experience in Kakuma seems to have imbued Samuel with a deep appreciation of good health, happiness, and compassion. "The United Nations wanted to make sure that we'd have a better future," he says. "Those of us who went through that [refugee experience] . . . we are very committed to life."

One of the organizations that played a pivotal role in the operation of the camp was the International Rescue Committee. In an article on the committee's website, Jason Phillips, manager of the IRC's programs in the early part of this century, described the importance of the help and guidance his organization extended to the Lost Boys: "The IRC's health, sanitation, community services, and education programs touched, in one way or another, the lives of all the Lost Boys who were in Kakuma and who were eventually resettled in the U.S.A. We accompanied and supported them throughout a large part of their journey."

Intercontinental Love and Romance

In 2001, the United States government stepped up and offered to bring nearly four thousand of the Lost Boys to America, paying their airfare, helping them find employment, and housing them in cities across the country. While the government required the refugees to repay the money for the airfare and housing, the relocation assistance did help them get a fresh start in living conditions they never could have imagined they'd ever experience. Many went on to graduate college, work solid jobs, get married, and raise families.

Samuel relocated to the Northeast and gained employment as a full-time certified nursing assistant at a prominent hospital, earning $14 an hour. Additionally, he enrolled in a registered nursing program and studied to become a nurse practitioner. "I had known for a long time that I wanted to do something with my life that involved helping people," he says. "I thought that would be a good contribution to America."

He also spent a lot of time corresponding with a young woman in Kenya named Esther, also a Sudanese teenage refugee, who he had met while growing up in Kenya. Before he relocated to the United States, the two agreed to keep in contact, the romance grew, and Samuel and Esther decided to marry. In January 2006, they exchanged vows in a civil wedding held in Kenya. That was a hallmark year for Samuel for another reason as well: Eleven months later, in November, he became a U.S. citizen. With plans to move Esther to the United States as soon as possible, he visited her in Kenya in early spring 2007, and, in December, their first child, a boy, was born in Kenya.

By 2009, the couple was more than ready to live in the same home on the same continent with their child and end the lengthy and costly cross-Atlantic treks to see one another. In May, Samuel filed an immigrant visa petition on behalf of his wife and son. But he had to take some important steps to move the process forward. First and foremost, because Samuel's son was a U.S. citizen by law, the U.S. consulate in Kenya requested that Samuel take a DNA test to prove paternity. He paid for the genetic test and submitted the results to the consulate. It was time-consuming and expensive—he had to fly to Nairobi to take the test in person—but relatively simple enough.

Yet week after week passed, and Samuel, eager to reunite his family in the U.S. Northeast, heard nothing from the consulate. Not a word. He waited several months and then contacted the consulate, which admitted that it had lost his DNA test results. Consulate officials told him his only course of action was to retake the test. On his time. With his money. In Kenya. He had no choice.

Consequently, Samuel once again took time off from work, paid for pricey airfare, and took the eighteen-hour flight back to Kenya for a repeat DNA test. As a result of his frequent travel, Samuel lost his full-time nursing job and was forced to find other work—a part-time health-care position at a nursing home, which paid him significantly less: under $11 an hour. With that considerable hit to his income, he struggled to support his family in Kenya but he did the best he could, and Esther appreciated his efforts.

The DNA test proved Samuel was indeed the father of his son, and, in October 2009, the government approved the petition for Samuel's wife and child. The consulate granted a passport to his young son and asked Esther to conduct an interview with immigration officials. Things were looking up . . . briefly. But the consulate did not schedule Esther's interview until the following year, in June 2010. Everything appeared to be on track. And then a full year later, in June 2011, the couple received horrible news: Esther received a notice that her visa application had been rejected.

A Tailspin of Missteps and Misdeeds

As it turns out, the rationale for the rejection centered on a chain reaction of several factors: an innocent email misfire that led to anger that escalated to malice that created an incredible case of mistaken identity that resulted in officials denying Esther's visa application, plunging the couple into despair. Here's what happened.

Like in some other nations, Sudan doesn't have a lot of variety of names. Samuel shared the same first, middle, and last names as another Sudanese Lost Boy who relocated in mid-2001 to a city in the Midwest, earned a master's degree, and married. A wonderful United States nonprofit organization had been monitoring and trying to help several of the Lost Boys, including both Samuel and Other Samuel. In good faith, a member of that nonprofit innocently misdirected an email containing personal information about Samuel's immigration case, including information about Esther, to Other Samuel, who replied and pointed out the mistake. I could see how easily such a slipup could happen, given the circumstances.

In his return email, Other Samuel mentioned that he was in the middle of a contentious and bitter divorce from his wife Olivia and that, somehow, she had gained access to his emails and may be reading them.

With an unknown motive but possibly thinking that her husband, Other Samuel, had illegally married and sponsored another woman while married to her, Olivia used the personal information and the case numbers contained in the errant email and contacted the U.S. consulate in Kenya. In a seemingly vengeful move that would fit right in with the character Glenn Close played in the famous movie *Fatal Attraction*, Olivia reported to the consulate that Samuel was, in fact, married to her and not to Esther. This was completely untrue, but because the husbands' names were the same, the consular officers believed her.

After learning of this horrific mix-up, the nonprofit group emailed the Immigrant Visa Unit in Nairobi, explaining that the rejection of Esther's visa application was based on incorrect information and described the circumstances of the mistaken identity. The consulate responded that they had received credible reports—which, of course, came from the angry informant, Olivia—that Samuel was married to and living with another woman. Consulate officials also said that, because of this, Samuel needed to produce evidence of a divorce.

A member of the nonprofit offered more details of the situation and produced a sworn affidavit that Samuel was never married to Olivia and that he knew them both. As if this were a plotline from a Theater of the Absurd performance, the consulate continued to demand evidence of divorce from a marriage that never happened.

Before I got involved in Samuel's case, several members of Congress had intervened on Samuel's behalf, arguing that Samuel's petition was wrongfully denied. Friends and people close to Samuel and Esther also submitted multiple affidavits. Despite the reams of documents submitted and the high-level congressional intervention, the case hit a dead end. The following March, the consulate sent Esther a letter stating that she was found ineligible for a visa because her husband is "married to another woman in [the] U.S." Samuel and Esther were crushed.

Samuel acknowledges just how frustrating, sad, and emotionally draining the experience was. "It was a very difficult time, being separated from my wife and son," he says. "It was tough, and I was crying sometimes, and I don't cry easily. It was difficult traveling back and forth to Africa. I tried so many things to get them here. I even talked to Congressmen."

Insensitive, Incompetent, and Intransigent Government

The nonprofit organization introduced me to Samuel, and we met in June 2012. I immediately liked him. Sitting next to me in our gleaming conference room, Samuel tried to tell me the story but broke down, crying on my shoulder. As I put my arm around him, my heart went out to this wonderful man, and I knew I had to help him overcome this nightmare. He's always polite, gentle, sweet yet very strong, and hardworking. On one hand, my team and I could hardly believe what he and Esther went through, but on the other hand, we knew that, too frequently, the government demonstrated this sort of incompetency, intransigence, and foot dragging, which generates confusion and sows injustice.

Too often, we see immigration officials acting insensitively, ignoring the harm they inflict on people. While most of these officers act appropriately, some are indifferent and even reckless in the way they handle—or fail to handle—their job responsibilities. Immigration candidates often endure so much hardship and sometimes life-threatening danger, and they don't deserve to be treated carelessly by the government, especially when, often, they do everything right on their end, taking all the steps required in the immigration process. The unnecessary, absurd roadblocks that Samuel faced in his legitimate efforts to be reunited with his wife and son were heartbreaking.

We prepared and filed a comprehensive advocacy package with the Ombudsman's Office of USCIS. The filing explained in passionate and strong language that Samuel had been the victim of a horrendous series of bureaucratic blunders and laid the case out in excruciating detail. In August 2012, two months after we worked to secure justice for Samuel and Esther, USCIS finally reaffirmed Samuel's immigrant visa petition for his wife and child, three very long years after the original approval. It helped, and continues to help, that the Mintz name carries cachet internationally when it comes to immigration law and other legal areas.

Life was looking good for the couple and even better when Esther gave birth to their second son in Kenya that same month.

And yet the story still had not mercifully come to a conclusion. Samuel attempted to schedule a final interview for Esther at the consulate, and, in response, officials there said no interview was available until April 2013. My team and I intervened again, directly with the U.S. consulate in Nairobi.

We wrote a forceful letter, sent it in an expensive, next-day airmail package, and I followed up with a phone call to the consulate. Our efforts succeeded, and we were able to expedite the final visa appointment. Soon thereafter, Esther finally received permanent residence status and the authorization to move with their children to the United States.

Since the time of their marriage, Esther and Samuel were forced to spend a total of seven years living on two different continents. After filing a valid immigrant visa petition, they spent four of these years waiting for the government to do what it should have done in the first place. Samuel's two children were one and five years old before the family was finally reunited.

A Frontline Worker during the COVID-19 Outbreak

They now have five children, and Esther works diligently as a cleaning woman at a local establishment. Samuel is living out his goal to contribute to the country he "loves very much" and help other people, working long hours in a major Northeast hospital as a clinical care technician. When COVID-19 hit his city hard and hospital intensive care beds filled to near capacity, he served in harm's way on the front lines day after day.

"My team and I work where we're needed throughout the hospital in post-op, recovery, pediatric, ICU, maternity, wherever the hospital needs our help," Samuel says. "It's been very difficult with COVID, and I do all that I can to protect myself and my family. It's frightening, but I do it because that's why I'm there doing that job."

He reflects on the surge in the outbreak in his community. "When we are on the job, we feel like we're on the front lines of a war," he says. "When you are fighting, you are focused on what you have to do. When we come home, we are hurting. But we have a lot of support in the community. People brought us food from local restaurants, and so many people told us they appreciate us and say, 'You guys are doing a wonderful job.' We work as a team."

When I asked Samuel if he would allow me to share his story in this book, he didn't hesitate to agree to participate, because, he says, so many people helped him and his family. He hopes that his message gets out: If you are lucky enough to come to this country, be grateful, seize opportunities, do your best to contribute to your communities, and help people when you can.

IN SUMMARY AND UPON REFLECTION:

IMMIGRANT BATTLES
ARE WORTHY OF THE FIGHT

While writing this book and recounting my clients' struggles and successes, I'm reminded of the pride that educator extraordinaire and Honduran immigrant José Salgado exhibited as he recalled talking to former students and learning of their career and personal achievements. Like José, I'm so proud of my clients' courage, fortitude, intelligence, creativity, pride in democracy, and passion for life.

I'm also grateful. I feel fortunate to have gotten to know them while handling their legal matters and then later, sometimes years later, as I hear about the lives they're leading, see them prosper, and in many cases, watch their children grow up as engaged American citizens.

For example, some twenty-five years ago, I represented a wonderful but desperate man who was forced to escape an African country after being brutally persecuted for standing up for the civil and human rights of members of his community. He was a husband and father of five children, but as in so many similar cases, he had to flee alone, on short notice, to survive. He left behind a professional high-level job and arrived in the U.S. practically penniless. As he was completely alone in a strange country, my family and I opened our home to him, and for years he was a regular guest at our dinner table on Friday nights. We were successful in winning his case, and many years later, after very lengthy administrative immigration processing, we secured the approval of the applications of his wife and five kids to come to the United States and finally reunite with him.

I'll never forget the day my husband, Michael, our sons, Gabe and Noah, and I brought him to the airport to be reunited with his wife and five young children. We watched his lovely wife and their wide-eyed youngsters emerge from the international arrivals section of the airport. She radiated elation, so happy and grateful to be here with her family. Their reunion was a profound and deeply emotional moment for all of us.

An immensely talented and highly educated woman, she already had several degrees before she got to the States. Once here, she dedicated herself to raising their children to rise to their utmost potential, working two jobs as a health aide with barely any time to rest and earning the income the family needed to afford tutors so each of the kids could get the support they needed to excel in school. This dignified, upstanding, hardworking woman not only raised their children to be straight-A students who won college scholarships, prizes, and awards, but she also went back to school herself—twice—while working two full-time jobs.

In the last several years, she has added two more degrees to her collection. She now holds four professional degrees and works as a nurse on the front lines of COVID-19. Their kids are grown and fully American now, and they're the epitome of immigrant success stories. All of them are college educated and are launching or planning promising professional careers. The eldest, a brilliant A+ student who won scholarships both to college and medical school, is a third-year medical resident at one of the country's top hospitals.

This second-generational success and the desire that children of immigrants have to give back to their communities happen often, and it's not surprising. After all, the children learn by example as they see their parents working diligently and offering support to others, while placing a high value on the virtues of education.

The eleven people featured in this book are, of course, only a very small but diverse sample of those my colleagues at Mintz Levin and I have served over the past thirty-five-plus years. I've represented thousands of immigrants from nearly every country in the world. While I've helped them navigate the arduous, complex maze of the immigration system—and done what I could to support them in many other ways—I feel I've been the fortunate one, a true beneficiary of these relationships. They've come into my life and have given me a window into their lives, their cultural identities, and their worldviews.

Michael, Gabe, and Noah have also benefited greatly. Our sons have been presented with and seized the opportunity to meet many of the wonderful people we've opened our home to and eaten dinner with around our table. Together, we've celebrated many momentous events in their lives or their children's lives. Through these experiences, I know that Noah and Gabe have seen, appreciated, and empathized with the struggles immigrants encounter. Our boys, now young men, have expanded their own worldviews by engaging with my clients. And I believe they'd be the first ones to say that they're better people for it.

As I've tried to convey in this book, the United States is also a better country because of the contributions immigrants have made and continue to make in so many ways: culturally, socially, politically, scientifically, medically, and economically. In fact, immigrants contribute to and strengthen the U.S. economy on farmlands, in small towns, suburbs, and particularly in our nation's cities. "Immigrants have mainly increased population and employment in large, densely populated urban areas, where productivity is much higher than elsewhere—contributing to increases in U.S. productivity and income per person," according to Giovanni Peri, a renowned economist and professor–chair of the Department of Economics at the University of California, Davis. "Regardless of education level, just by increasing the overall size of the economy, immigrants have produced a proportional growth of the nation's gross domestic product."[1] And a 2020 study published by scholars at the Kellogg School of Management at Northwestern University confirms the "dual roles of immigrants as founders and workers." The findings suggest that immigrants act more as "job creators" than "job takers" and that non-U.S.-born founders play outsized roles in U.S. high-growth entrepreneurship.[2]

These are just a few of the scholarly assessments among many. Immigrants come here, pay taxes, and work hard, often creating and building businesses that provide well-paying jobs, generate revenues and profits, and enhance our communities. I've seen this firsthand with so many of my clients, including Tony Tjan.

The son of overseas Chinese–Indonesian parents who immigrated into Canada from Asia, Tony grew up on the far easterly edge of North America in Newfoundland. He attended and graduated from Harvard with an AB degree in biology, going on to earn an MBA at Harvard Business School, serve as a fellow at the Harvard Kennedy School of Government, and become a member of the Advisory Council of the MIT Media Lab. He has forged an illustrious career as an entrepreneur, an investor, and a strategic advisor.

I met Tony in late 1997, when he contacted me for help in securing a work visa for one of the cofounders of his start-up company, ZEFER, an innovative internet advisory firm. I also helped him gain his own work visa and eventually a green card; he became an American citizen in 2013. ZEFER is a prime example of an immigrant-run success story that was pioneering during the earliest days of the internet's commercialization.

---

1   Peri, G., & Cicala, S. (2018, October 16). Immigration and Economic Growth in the U.S., 2000–2015. Econofact. https://econofact.org/immigration-and-economic-growth-in-the-u-s-2000-2015.

2   Azoulay, P., Jones, B., Kim, J. D., & Miranda, J. (2020, September 7). Immigration and Entrepreneurship in the United States. NBER. https://www.nber.org/papers/w27778.

The firm opened trail-blazing opportunities for people and businesses in the dot-com world by harnessing the many ways that "being digital" (to quote Nicholas Negroponte) could change the way the world works and the way we live. In a short time, the company grew in both revenues and size and had secured one of the largest rounds of early-stage venture funding at the time (over $100 million), which allowed it to grow its workforce to nearly 1000 people. While the company had to navigate the ups and downs of the dot-com economy, it eventually sold in late 2001 to the large Japanese conglomerate NEC, which it remains a part of today.

After ZEFER, Tony went on to serve as the senior advisor to the CEO of the Thomson Corporation (now Thomson Reuters) (one of his clients at ZEFER) and worked side by side with him for more than seven years, playing a key role in helping lead one of the largest transformations in media. The shift took a traditional newspaper and a diversified holding company to become a leading global provider of critical information services—a $30 billion multinational media conglomerate, Thomson Reuters.

Along the way, Tony also became a *New York Times* bestselling author and a 2018 recipient of the Ellis Island Medal of Honor, which recognizes our nation's immigrant heritage, in addition to individual achievement. Part of the recognition for his work was for how he is using capital as a force for purposeful investing and positive change.

Through his venture capital company, Cue Ball, Tony has invested in and has grown scores of successful companies. Through his efforts, he has not only stimulated the economy of the U.S.; he's improved the working environments and labor conditions of so many of these companies. A case in point: He cofounded and backed MiniLuxe, a lifestyle brand that seeks to elevate and transform the $45 billion nail care industry. MiniLuxe started with the goal of "Starbucking the nail salon industry" and has, over the past decade, been able to establish cleaner and ethical standards for treatments and products that have traditionally been unsafe for employees and clients. Perhaps most important and from the perspective of passing on "immigrant success," he has been central to the company's commitment to uplifting the educational and fair work practices of the largest vocational class of women workers (nail technicians) who happen to be largely immigrant based and predominantly Asian American. The brand has been resilient in surviving the COVID-19 pandemic and resolute about maintaining its standards and supporting its team members. Today, MiniLuxe has locations in a growing number of states across the country and trains and employs hundreds of nail designers in a safer and more nurturing environment, offering real career growth and economic mobility. By his estimate, Cue Ball and its partners have invested over $100 million toward inclusionary ventures during the past decade, which, in addition to MiniLuxe, includes several women- and minority-led ventures.

My client Joydeep Bhattacharyya is another example of a brilliant venture capitalist who is an engine of economic growth, fueling the creation of important jobs in our country. Joydeep has a degree in computer science and engineering from his native country of India, as well as an MBA from the Kellogg School of Management at Northwestern University, where he was a fellow at the Center for Research in Technology and Innovation. Joydeep's software engineering genius manifests in everything he does. After a spectacular career in India, Joydeep relocated to the United States. Here, he served as a key member of the team that conceived, designed, and patented Microsoft Office 365, as well as Microsoft's Skype for Business (Microsoft Office's web conferencing component).

After working in a series of highly influential engineering roles, Joydeep pivoted to the world of venture capital in Silicon Valley. He invests in and advises early-stage American companies that provide software to manage internet connected devices in large enterprises. Applying his remarkable engineering acumen and penetrating analysis to help American start-ups and early-stage companies, Joydeep is uniquely positioned to help the United States drive innovation in software and technology.

It's impossible to overstate the value and importance of Joydeep's contributions to the United States and the benefits we all reap from his presence here. For example, one of his venture capital company's recent investments is in a U.S. company that secures essential infrastructure such as electrical grids, oil refineries, and gas pipelines. It's certainly in our best interests as a country, and a great comfort to me, to know that Joydeep supports and guides the design and implementation of such sophisticated software to guard against cyberattacks on our essential infrastructure.

Countless American companies and millions of U.S. consumers have benefited from Joydeep's expertise. With his strategic guidance, many of the companies Joydeep has taken under his wing have received national attention, achieved significant commercial success, and hired large numbers of American workers, directly benefiting the U.S. economy and strengthening U.S. competitiveness in the global economy.

I've served innumerable immigrants who, like Tony and Joydeep, are job creators who have grown incredible companies that transform industries and create useful products and health-care solutions that improve Americans' lives, and fuel and strengthen the U.S. economy.

A Tough Row to Hoe

But as this book demonstrates, the success immigrants attain doesn't come without a great deal of toil, tears, and trauma, and often sweat and blood as well. Just think of the long and treacherous journeys that some of the immigrants portrayed in these pages had to take to flee the horrific conditions and often dangerous circumstances they faced in their homelands. Many of these escapes began on foot. Gazmend Kapplani risked being shot when he walked with trepidation past armed border guards to leave his native totalitarian country. Peng Xu hiked over the Burmese mountains to flee the dangers he faced in China. With thousands of other Lost Boys of Sudan, Samuel Bol walked 1000 miles in a perilous trek to a refugee camp in Kenya. Audrey Uwimana literally ran for her life from Rwanda to Uganda.

Then, when immigrants reach the United States, they must embark on another journey, jumping over the many bureaucratic hurdles of the complex and, in many ways, broken U.S. immigration system—a system that too often lets immigrants down. The clients I worked with followed the letter and spirit of the immigration laws, regulations, and procedures and did everything right over the course of a years-long process—or in the case of Jacque Colon, two decades—to live permanently in this country. It's a tricky legal tightrope they all must traverse because the government makes it very difficult for them to avoid running afoul of the law and risking deportation.

For example, among the hundreds of changes President Trump proposed to our immigration system was that asylum-seekers, after filing for asylum, would have to wait more than a year to apply for a work authorization card that would allow them to work in this country legally. This means it would be at least eighteen months before they'd have the work card in their hands to show to a potential employer. And yet, if a person works without proper work authorization, they're deportable. How is a person supposed to survive in this country without working? Gotcha! This is but one of countless examples of how lawmakers and bureaucrats manipulate the immigration system to ensnare immigrants and trip them up.

Immigrants, as well as American citizens, sometimes have to deal with incompetent and occasionally mean-spirited government employees. I've been privileged to meet and work closely with so many admirable officers at all of the various agencies that deal with U.S. immigration. These hardworking folks perform their jobs professionally and honorably and do all they can to help immigrants. But I've also seen bad actors terribly mistreat immigrants and poison the immigration experience, giving our country a bad reputation and leaving a very sour taste in the mouths of those who've suffered mistreatment at their hands. One of my own colleagues, an American citizen, was returning from an overseas trip and standing in line at U.S. immigration a few years ago (during President

Trump's time in office). He observed the Customs and Border Protection officer yelling at and berating an immigrant who was standing in line right in front of him. My colleague had previously served at a very high level in our federal government, and he understood how important it is for the United States to welcome visitors and encourage trade and commerce with the United States. For the millions of people who come to our nation every year, our immigration and customs officers are the very first Americans they meet, and first impressions really matter. He spoke up and told the male officer, "As someone who, like you, has served in federal government, I strongly believe that you should speak respectfully to the people you inspect at our borders; it reflects poorly on our country when our government officials act so rudely when performing their jobs." In a rage, the officer immediately took my colleague out of line, roughly put him into an interrogation room, and went into the CBP computer system and rescinded my colleague's Global Entry authorization—just because my colleague spoke up for a fellow human being. I had to go to the head of the Global Entry Program in Washington, DC, to get his authorization reinstated, and still it took three months to sort it out. For most people who do not have the kind of relationships that I have developed, it's unlikely this type of vindictive government overstepping would be redressed.

It's hard to believe that such an outrageous abuse of authority could take place in a country like the United States. Sadly, such encounters are more common than one might think. Unfortunately, many talented immigrants who've voluntarily moved away from the United States have told me that a particularly nasty or rude encounter with an immigration officer at an airport or at the border pushed them to the decision to seek their fortunes in a different country. After hearing each of these stories, I always feel embarrassed, and I apologize to them on behalf of my country for the disrespectful treatment they endured. While most of our government officials act appropriately, we must be vigilant to call out abuses of authority when they happen.

Over the decades, lawmakers and agency regulators have sought to implement legal reforms to improve our complex immigration system, with varying degrees of success. As I have noted, in my career, I've not seen anything like the cruelty toward immigrants or the erosion of the rule of law that occurred over the four years of the Trump administration. Under the direction of President Trump, our immigration agencies indiscriminately terrorized and rounded up enormous numbers of immigrants, filling our jails and detention centers to overflowing levels. These xenophobic, cruel, and often inhumane measures frequently violated the sacred tenets of our Constitution and stand in opposition to the philosophy embodied by the Statue of Liberty, which I believe represents the truly American value of welcoming immigrants to our land—both those who are prosperous and those who are downtrodden and yearning to breathe free. We not only have room in our country to accommodate a robust immigration system, but we'll stagnate and become a poorer country culturally and economically if we close our doors and our hearts to immigrants.

The former president's infamous vitriolic rhetoric against immigrants, among other unsettling dynamics, has created a toxic atmosphere in which xenophobia flourishes. Additionally, economic downturns or even economic instabilities often unleash hateful words and deeds. During my career, I've seen the ebbs and flows of xenophobia during economic cycles. In tight times, people worry about their financial well-being and often perceive that those who are foreign born threaten their jobs, their livelihoods. These perceptions are unfounded and supported by no solid statistical evidence by independent labor and economic experts. Yet they continue to persist.

The combination of erroneous perceptions, bigoted attitudes, hateful words, and harmful political actions fuels violence against and mass shootings of American-born minorities and immigrants. Think Charlottesville in 2017 or El Paso in 2019 or Atlanta in 2021 or the spike in hate crimes against innocent people that began to surge fifteen or sixteen years into the twenty-first century.

Speaking of innocent people, I think it's extremely important to address another common misperception. In too many countries around the world, the people who are arrested and thrown in jail—sometimes without due process or even a trial—didn't actually commit a crime. Furthermore, many of the crimes with which these people have been charged are based on trumped-up charges or illegitimate grounds by corrupt governments. Of course, some who attempt to enter the United States are indeed criminals, but to make blanket statements suggesting that all or most immigrants are murderers, rapists, and thieves—as many people do, including U.S. leaders and former leaders—is flat-out wrong and downright dangerous. I've heard people say that immigrants with criminal records, including those seeking political asylum here who may have a so-called criminal record, are "bad people, and we don't want them here."

While I'd be the first to agree that we can't have an open-door policy that allows in everyone regardless of their criminal record, it's important not to conflate all crimes or arrest records. Many of the asylum-seekers I've represented stood up for democracy in their countries, and as a result of their peaceful protests, they were arrested, imprisoned, and tortured by dictatorial regimes run by thugs and brutal secret police forces. So yes, they have arrest records. But they're the farthest thing from criminals; they're heroes. And sometimes, immigrants have no choice but to obtain false documents to escape for their lives. These people also aren't criminals. Those I've had the good fortune to meet are intelligent, creative, compassionate people of the highest moral character. They should be embraced, not rejected and vilified.

Our immigration laws contain so many misguided provisions, but perhaps one of the worst is the inclusion of misdemeanor convictions in the definition of *aggravated felonies* (such as theft of an item as inexpensive as a cell phone charger, if the applicable state law would impose a sentence of at least one year for a conviction). Non–United States citizens who are convicted of a crime labeled by the U.S. Congress as an aggravated felony are ineligible for almost any form of immigration relief, and every year, thousands of immigrants who've been harshly branded with this wrong-headed moniker are deported, without regard to their rehabilitation or subsequent contributions to our society. It should be a priority for our Congress to reform this unduly overbroad and disproportionately harsh *aggravated felony* definition.

Call to Action

Fortunately, I've also met many people who do embrace immigrants, recognize the societal and economic value they bring to this country, and ask me, "What can I do to help?" Well, here are a few things I tell them, and if it's important to you to support and protect the rights of immigrants and work to strengthen the rule of law in the United States, I encourage you to help too.

Craft Connections

If you have an immigrant friend or acquaintance and you also know someone who doesn't know any immigrants, try to make an introduction. Invite them both to lunch, and have them get to know one another. Or even better, you could host a dinner party where people can meet others from different cultures, hear their stories, and learn about their contributions to the United States. Often, people don't have the means of meeting other people who they'd never engage with socially. You can connect people and see human commonalities, emotions, and laughter play out before you.

Create a Venue

Host another type of get-together where an immigrant can tell their story to a group of people. It will likely open the eyes of those people to a world they'd not seen before. An excellent venue for this is at your place of worship if your congregation leader is supportive of the idea—especially during the month of June, which is World Refugee Month. If the immigrant you know doesn't want to speak in front of a large group of people, perhaps their immigration lawyer can share the person's story with their permission.

Donate Time
Volunteer for a local nonprofit that serves immigrants—even short stints of volunteerism can make a difference.

Write for Change
If you're particularly moved by the contributions of someone you know who's an immigrant or the struggles they've faced, with their permission, draft and submit a letter to the editor or an op-ed article to a newspaper or online media outlet. It might just change readers' minds.

Vote for Change
Support candidates who appreciate the contribution immigrants make, advance policies that protect their rights, and work to improve the immigration process.

Start Conversations
Ask an immigrant what they did before they came here, if it's not uncomfortable to do so. You'll find that so many immigrants were very accomplished in their countries, and now they're cleaning office buildings, driving Ubers, and working all kinds of jobs that are worthy and serve a purpose but don't necessarily reflect their education and expertise.

Lend a Hand
Help an immigrant with their resume; take steps to mentor them.

Build Networks
Make introductions for them in the business world.

Invest in Compassion

Donate financially to organizations like PAIR (www.pairproject.org) and to other nonprofit organizations that support immigrants.

Spark Thoughtfulness

If you know someone who is opposed to immigrants, gently ask that person if they would be willing to share their own family's immigration story with you. Most of us in this country are the descendants of immigrants. If it is not too uncomfortable to do so, ask them where they think they might be today if their ancestors had not immigrated to the United States.

Show Appreciation

Tell an immigrant you're glad and grateful they're here. It seems so simple—and it is—but it's very important and makes a huge difference in an immigrant's life. And when you meet one, thank an immigration lawyer for his or her contributions to pursuing justice and immigrants' legal rights in this country; we all benefit when our rule of law is strengthened.

In Closing

I've showcased the amazing immigration and life journeys of these eleven clients and the bumpy and twisting legal paths they have traversed to bring their American immigration dreams to fruition. As we've seen, many had to walk for hundreds of miles before they could even reach our shores. I hope this book has allowed you to "walk a mile in their shoes" and has brought you closer to them and to every American immigrant's journey.

ABOUT THE AUTHORS

Susan J. Cohen

Susan is recognized as one of the top immigration lawyers in the United States. As Founding Chair of Mintz's Immigration Practice, she works with corporate clients to address their immigration challenges, with foreign-born company founders and entrepreneurs and with individuals from all over the world who seek her counsel on urgent matters. For over three decades Susan has chaired and co-chaired a wide range of committees of the American Immigration Lawyers Association (AILA) and the American Bar Association (ABA) and has contributed to significant federal and state immigration regulations.

With her team of 35 attorneys, specialists, and assistants in the Mintz immigration department she founded and oversees, Susan collaborates with corporate and individual clients to address the array of immigration challenges they encounter every day. She helps companies navigate around immigration obstacles, enabling them to bring in the creative international talent they need, grow their market share by seizing opportunities, and do what they do best: run their businesses, provide good jobs, and enhance their communities.

Susan closely monitors proposed modifications to the ever-evolving regulatory framework governing immigration. This enables her to foresee changes coming, prepare for them, and then move quickly to advise and protect her clients when measures and decisions by the executive branch, Congress, or the judiciary alter the immigration landscape.

Taking a lead in the firm's steadfast commitment to community service and pro bono work, Susan has helped many immigrants obtain asylum. Often this requires her to collaborate closely with asylum candidates to gather and organize voluminous evidence for their cases; reach out to government officials and others with whom she has cultivated strong working relationships; and use her strong persuasive communications skills to craft airtight cases to present to judges and other immigration decision makers.

Susan has won awards for her political asylum work from the Supreme Judicial Court of Massachusetts, the Rian Immigrant Center, the Political Asylum/Immigration Representation Project (PAIR), the Massachusetts Lawyers Weekly, and others.

Frequently quoted in the media, Susan also accepts many invitations to speak to a variety of audiences at public events. She regularly writes on immigration law topics and serves on the Editorial Board of Law360. She also serves as an editor of Mintz's Immigration Law blog and has been recognized as a "Top Author" by JD Supra.

A frequent conference panelist and public speaker, she also contributes thought leadership to immigration publications and the popular press.

Steven T. Taylor

Steven T. Taylor is an award-winning journalist and writer who has written more than 900 articles, editorials, essays, and other works on such subjects as law, politics, leadership, the environment, art, and business for more than sixty publications and organizations, including *The Nation, The Washington Post, Washington City Paper, The Washington Times, The National Jurist, Cascadia Times, Willamette Week, Environmental Protection News, Environmental Protection Magazine, E: The Environmental Magazine, Technology Transfer Business, Of Counsel, ABA's Law Practice, American City & County,* CBS News, The Center for Public Integrity, Public Citizen, Chronicle Publications, Content Pilot, and Voice of the Environment.

He's also coauthor with Dudley R. Slater of the book *Fusion Leadership: Unleashing the Movement of Monday Morning Enthusiasts* (Greenleaf Book Group Press, 2017), an Amazon bestseller in its category.

Steve wrote the investigative study *Sleeping with the Industry: The U.S. Forest Service and Timber Interests,* published by The Center for Public Integrity, and the report *CHAINSAW JUSTICE: The U.S. Forest Service Out of Control,* published by Voice of the Environment. Both of these 80-plus-page reports were released at press conferences at the National Press Club in Washington and gained significant media attention. He also wrote the investigative report *De-ranged: The Bureau of Land Management and the Plight of the American West.*

His article on the possible dangers of carpet chemicals, which originally appeared in Public Citizen Health Research Group's *Health Letter,* was honored as one of the top 25 news stories of 1993 not covered by the mainstream media in *CENSORED: The News That Didn't Make the News and Why,* by Carl Jensen & Project Censored. He's also a recipient of the Washington Press Club Foundation Award.

As one of two on-site staff writers, Steve wrote much of the *New York Times* bestselling history book *Chronicle of the 20th Century* (Chronicle Publications, 1987, American Booksellers Association book of the year), including all of the articles on the environment and most of the stories on civil rights, World War II, the Vietnam War, and national political events.

A retired college professor, Steve taught nonfiction writing and public presentation at the Oregon College of Art and Craft for 22 years.

Steve has two grown children he's very proud of, 24-year-old Perry and 21-year-old Julia, and lives with his wife of 26 years and best friend, Cindy, in Portland, Oregon.

CPSIA information can be obtained
at www.ICGtesting.com
Printed in the USA
LVHW102300081121
702820LV00015B/1030